PRAISE FOR *THE RIGHTEOUS PATH*

"Mention noir and the typical mystery reader thinks of the mean streets of Los Angeles or New York, but *The Righteous Path* is anything but typical. It's the story of rural West Virginia Sheriff Matt Simms, who's battling a deadly illness while trying to keep peace and security in a noir-ish part of America that's been overlooked and forgotten by society. Exquisitely written and filled with crisp dialogue and observations, *The Righteous Path* is one not to be missed."

—Brendan DuBois, award-winning and *New York Times* bestselling author

"Shamus winner James D.F. Hannah expertly delivers a mystery with more switchback twists than a mountain road, peppered with characters readers will enjoy taking this wild ride with. I dare you to try to put this book down."

—LynDee Walker, Amazon Charts bestselling author of *No Sin Unpunished*

"In *The Righteous Path*, James D.F. Hannah mixes ricochet banter and raw humanity to create a page-turning mystery. I have some catching up to do!"

—Award-winning author J.D. Allen

THE RIGHTEOUS PATH

BOOKS BY JAMES D.F. HANNAH

The Henry Malone novels
Midnight Lullaby
Complicated Shadows
She Talks To Angels
Friend of the Devil
Behind the Wall of Sleep

The Parker County novels
The Righteous Path

JAMES D.F. HANNAH

THE RIGHTEOUS PATH

A Parker County Novel

Copyright © 2019 by James D.F. Hannah
First Down & Out Books Edition July 2021

All rights reserved. No part of the book may be reproduced in any form or by any electronic or mechanical means, including information storage and retrieval systems, without permission in writing from the publisher, except by a reviewer who may quote brief passages in a review.

Down & Out Books
3959 Van Dyke Road, Suite 265
Lutz, FL 33558
DownAndOutBooks.com

The characters and events in this book are fictitious. Any similarity to real persons, living or dead, is coincidental and not intended by the author.

Cover design by Eric Beetner

ISBN: 1-64396-174-8
ISBN-13: 978-1-64396-174-3

*To Messrs. McBain and Parker,
without whom I might have never written a word.
Your stories will long inspire.*

Chapter 1

Diggtown was an unincorporated part of Parker County, outside Serenity city limits, so it fell under the sheriff's department jurisdiction. Once upon a time, it had been a coal camp built to house workers. The narrow road reflected the history, lined on both sides by identical A-frames, one right after another. *Boom, boom, boom, boom.*

Ask people and they'd tell you this shit never used to happen. Neighbors stayed tight then. Everyone kept an eye on each other. You caught the neighbor's kid doing something he wasn't supposed to be doing, you didn't think twice about breaking a switch and laying a beating on the kid's ass. Try that now and you'd have cops knocking at your door. End up in court for laying hands on someone's precious angel. All of it ignoring how the little demon had a puppy tied to a tree, half a gallon of gasoline, a box of matches, and a smile that implied the kid would hit full-fledged psycho mode before he had a high school diploma in his hands. Yeah, those days were long gone, folks. What you got in its place, you got shit like tonight.

The coal companies sold the A-frames years ago, and now the homes sat in various states. Some wore fresh paint, flowers in the front yard, kept the lawn mowed. Might be a loose shingle or two, but there were still the signs someone took time and cared, still had a sense of pride. Other houses hardly qualified as shacks, tumbling toward oblivion. Weeds up to the waist bloomed like actual flowers. Windows busted out, paint chipped and faded away to nothing. Year after year of coal dust filled cracked wood and made houses seem filthy in a way a power washer and five coats of paint would never fix.

Now, you didn't even know the name of whoever lived next to you anymore. You weren't supposed to, everyone wanting to be left alone. You didn't watch over your neighbor, and they sure as hell didn't watch over you. You got told to mind your own goddamn business—you knew what was fucking good for you.

It's a different world, Sheriff Matt Simms thought as he pulled the cruiser into the driveway.

He had been in bed when Crash called, the cell phone breaking his concentration as he stared at the bedroom ceiling, Rachel snoring next to him. He had been tired but couldn't sleep. Where was the justice in that?

Crash only told him it was "bad." Crash, only a few years out of college—little more than a kid in Matt's mind—didn't seem to have any true gauge on what qualified as bad. Matt—sitting in his second term as sheriff, and an MP before that during a stint with Uncle Sam—he understood bad. *Bad* was the teddy bear on the side of the road next to a three-car pileup. *Bad* was explaining to a man how his wife ended up dead in a motel with a syringe hanging out of her arm. *Bad* was seeing a couple realize now they had grandchildren to raise and funerals to plan.

Matt dressed in jeans and a sheriff's department polo shirt. He cinched the belt to the last notch, and the jeans still hung loose on his frame. Nothing fit anymore. He wondered if he needed to break down, buy new clothes.

He shook his head. Nope. Refused. He figured there were only two outcomes for his situation: either shit would get fixed and he'd put the weight back on, and everything would fit again, or it wouldn't get fixed, and the last bit of clothing he would need to buy would be the suit for his funeral. Either way, he couldn't justify paying fifty bucks for new jeans.

He kissed Rachel on the forehead before he left. She never stirred. It was just after midnight.

There were two sheriff's cruisers already parked across the street. The deputies had parked there so Matt could pull up into the driveway, so he wouldn't have far to walk. He hated that.

Charlotte "Crash" Landing came out the front of the house as Matt closed the cruiser door. Twenty-five, she could have been Matt's daughter. Short and wiry, Crash wore her dark hair just long enough for a ponytail. She looked no-nonsense, dark eyes focused and intense, more intimidating than her size implied, and she used it to her advantage. She was local, with a degree in criminology from WVU, but she bypassed the state police option. Came straight from college and applied for an open position with the sheriff's department.

It was only a six-person department, and even though she had less seniority than every other deputy, it was agreed when Matt selected a new chief deputy, that Crash was the best option. Part of that may have been because no one wanted to deal with the extra paperwork that came with the job, whereas Crash had boundless enthusiasm for the minutiae that drove everyone else nuts.

Matt was halfway up the sidewalk when Crash met him and said, "We've got this if you want to go on back home."

"The hell you say. You don't drag a man from bed, the middle of the night, then send him home. I was content laying and listening to my wife snore."

"Rachel snores?"

"Used to be worse. Probably used to it now. The key to a good marriage is overlooking the shit that would drive you crazy if they were anyone else."

"You should write a book, offer up advice of that sort."

"I believe people would profit from my wisdom and years of

experience." Matt looked toward the house. "Ambulance take 'em already?"

"Right before you got here." Crash flipped open a notebook. "Their names are Gary and Wilma Campbell. Both early seventies. They came home from a meeting at church. From the look of it, the perps—"

"'Perps?'"

"Yeah, perps. Perpetrators."

"I know what it means; I just never heard anyone use the term before who wasn't Dennis Franz."

"What do you suggest I call them?"

"There's plenty of choice words but none we can type into a report. But please continue."

"Anyway, the perps—" Crash paused for a beat, letting the word hang there, then shrugged and soldiered on. "It looks like they came in through the rear entrance. Busted the doorknob off of the back door. They tore the place up before the Campbells got home."

"Either of the Campbells able to talk?"

"No. Someone called 911 and Tim caught the call."

Tim Martin was a deputy who handled night duties five nights out of seven. Divorced, no kids, didn't mind being out all night. He didn't talk much. Seemed to like the solitude.

"Anyone see anything?" Matt said.

"Haven't had a chance to start a canvass, but I wouldn't want to put money on the possibility. This late at night, no one pays attention to what's going on next door."

"Once upon a time, someone would have been."

Crash pointed to the house on the other side of the road. It was a mirror image of where she and Matt stood, except no lights on inside, the grass overgrown, "No Trespassing" signs posted on the fence.

"World's not 1955 anymore," she said. "It's not *Leave It to Beaver*, or whatever you people watched. People want left alone."

"I get it. I don't have to like it, though."

THE RIGHTEOUS PATH

Matt followed Crash inside. Matt guessed the place looked the same way it had for thirty, forty years. The furniture might have changed out at some point—the couch seemed like it had cost a penny or two around a few decades ago—but otherwise it had been a house in stasis. Until tonight.

The living room furniture had been ripped open and its insides pulled out, foam and stuffing all over the floor and couch. Photographs of grandchildren had been yanked from walls and the glass shattered. A bowling ball rested inside the frame of an ancient console TV. Matt noticed pools of blood drying into the carpet.

Broken shards of dishes were scattered across the kitchen linoleum. The wooden handles of knives jutted out of the wall as if from a circus act. Brown streaks were smeared around it.

Matt sniffed and made a face. "Jesus, that's what I think it is, isn't it?"

"There's urine on the hallway carpet," Crash said. She gestured at the brown streaks. "We're thinking feces and not chocolate icing."

Matt rubbed at his chin with a balled fist. "Tim called the paramedics when he came on scene?"

"Yes. He found the Campbells unresponsive. Mrs. Campbell was unconscious in the living room, so probably that's her blood in there. Mr. Campbell was here in the kitchen. He had the phone in his hand when we found him."

"What do we know about the Campbells?"

"Mr. Campbell's retired. Owned a group of local grocery stores until the big chains made it too much to keep that up, so he closed 'em seven or eight years ago."

"What about family? Kids? Photos looked like there are grandkids."

"We found an address book next to the base for the cordless phone and called a daughter in Ohio."

"How'd she sound?"

"Tim made the call, not me. He said the daughter didn't say

much. Asked if they were okay and said she'd be here in the morning."

Matt surveyed the scene. The more he looked at it all, the angrier he got. Enough years doing this, and the anger never went away. "It won't do much, but we'll need to canvass the neighbors. Maybe someone's got a security camera that recorded something, or they've got a weak bladder and had to get up to piss, or the dog needed let out. Something."

"We'll get on it, Matt."

They walked back outside. Matt sucked in lungfuls of cool night air, trying to push out the fetid stink. He leaned against the house, head resting on the wall, eyes closed.

Crash stood there without a word.

"How you feeling?" she said.

Eyes still closed, Matt said, "Fucking perfection. Couldn't be better."

"Talk to Carl?"

Matt's eyes flickered open. "The other day."

"How's he doing?"

"About however you would expect him to be doing. He's at his most Carl-like state."

Crash smiled. "That has to be exhausting."

"Mostly for his sister."

"He still living with her?"

"Until his place gets fixed up. A wheelchair ramp, rework the bathroom, things like that. All accessibility issues."

"Tell him if he needs anything, we're there."

"I will."

"You think he's gonna want to talk to any of us anytime soon?"

"His call, not mine, and it'll be on his time, no one else's. Takes time, Crash. Carl's a proud man." Matt pushed himself upright, flat onto his feet. "I've got a doctor's appointment first thing, so I'll be late coming in."

"We can handle things from here."

"I know you can."
"Go home, Matt. Listen to Rachel snore."
Matt nodded and got into his cruiser.

Chapter 2

Under normal circumstances, the nurse made Matt put on one of those ridiculous gowns—the one with the open back and the tie around his neck and his ass showing to the world—but this was just a follow-up, talking over test results from the previous week's blood work, so he got to keep on his jeans and black button-up with "Parker County Sheriff's Department" sewn into the chest.

He sat in the exam room, hands on his legs, looking at the wall. He wished he could be someone able to kill time staring at a cell phone: flinging birds across ravines, battling warring societies, liking photos of last night's dinner. Hell, he still had a flip phone. Phone calls and text messages. Simple and functional.

Though when waiting in the exam room, having a way to murder the minutes that dragged their asses across the floor would have been nice. Instead, Matt listened to the hum of the nurses outside chattering away about the TV show from the night before, asking about the new cardiovascular surgeon and if he was single, and complaining because of the new paperwork the insurance companies required for billing.

When that got old, Matt turned to the methodical tick of the wall clock. The clock was a gimme from a pharmaceutical rep advertising a diabetes drug Matt knew was pulled off the market two years ago after it was traced back to a string of strokes in patients. Which, he guessed, had jack-shit to do with whether the clock itself kept accurate time. But still.

Dr. Fordham came in, manila folders tucked underneath his arm. Fordham was older than Matt, stocky with a bloom of white hair encircling his head, and a flat, twisted nose that might have gotten that way from a punch years ago. He wore wire-rimmed glasses and an expression like he was pissed off. He always looked that way, like all of life's little annoyances had come together to a rolling boil and he wasn't ready to dismiss a single fucking one of them.

Fordham plopped onto a small stool and rolled across the exam room until his knees almost met Matt's. In the time he had been seeing Fordham, Matt discovered the man lacked any concept of respect for personal space.

The doctor flipped open the top folder and tilted his head back, deepened his look of disgust, and closed the folder. He stared at Matt for seconds that seemed like days. Matt stared back. This was how it always played with the old man.

"Good news," Fordham said. "You're cured."

"Awesome," Matt said, half rising out of his chair. "It's been great to know you, Doc—"

"Sit your ass down. You're still riddled with cancer."

Matt collapsed back into his seat. "You have a hell of a way of dropping news on a patient."

"It's taken me years to develop this bedside manner. Don't make plans on me changing it soon."

Fordham opened the folder again and leafed through several pages. His face softened as he looked up at Matt.

"You ever a drinker?" Fordham said.

"No more than anyone else. The occasional beer and whatnot."

Fordham set the folder aside. "Which is why I'm fucking mystified by this. Because what you have is hepatocellular carcinoma, which you normally see in hepatitis B and C patients or morbidly obese diabetics, of which you're neither. While we caught it too far along for surgery to be an option, the chemo was holding it at bay. That window's closing now, though."

"Am I to presume that I'm still dying?"

"Yes. Faster than before, even. The cancer's becoming more aggressive, as if you pissed it off."

"I piss people off. Can't imagine it being any different for malignant cells."

"We need to get you moved up the donor's list as soon as possible. Your clock is ticking hard and fast."

Matt looked down at his hands. He remembered when they'd been strong and substantial. When he'd played football in the army. When he'd gone hunting on weekends, holding the weight of the rifle as he lined a buck up in his sights. When he lifted Rachel and carried her into the bedroom, and the way her body trembled with anticipation.

"How soon?" Matt said. "Before you can hook me up with a new liver?"

"I don't know," Fordham said. "You cut lines on these things, it's not like skipping the popcorn aisle at the movie theater. But I'll see what I can do."

"Thanks, Doc. I appreciate it."

"Not a problem. If you die, I don't want to dump my bill on Rachel."

"She thanks you for that, as well."

"How's she doing?"

"She's good. She takes it all in stride."

"I hope you lie better than that to other people."

Matt raised his open palms into the air as if swearing an oath. "She's doing how you'd think she was doing if you told anyone their husband was dying."

Fordham flipped through the manila folders. His finger traced a path down a sheet of lined notebook paper clipped to computer printouts. "You guys just got remarried, right?"

"Three months ago. Right before the diagnosis."

"Goddamn. Wasn't she married before that?"

"She was. We were, I mean. Married. We divorced a few

years back, and she got married to an attorney."

"She left that to come back to your sorry cancer-filled ass?"

"And here I thought it was just my liver with the cancer. Great. But so you know, the attorney cheated on her. Plus, he was laundering drug money for white supremacists."

"Nonetheless, she still left him for you?"

"In my defense, I wasn't filled with cancer then." Matt gave his neck a gentle twist, listening for the crack. There was a small, subtle pop. "Is this the attitude you take with all of your patients?"

Fordham pulled the glasses off his face. Matt thought the doctor had the face of an aging boxer, or perhaps a dog with a shoved-up snout, the ones everyone called "so ugly they're cute."

"Just the ones I like," Fordham said.

"And the ones you don't like, do they accept death as the preferable option?"

For the first time since Fordham had walked into the exam room, he smiled.

"Who would want to give up all of this charm?"

Chapter 3

Crash called Matt as he left the doctor's office to tell him Mr. Campbell was awake. She waited for him in the hospital parking lot, holding a cup of convenience store coffee in each hand. She offered one cup to him. Matt popped the lid off and took a long drink. Crash watched with wide eyes.

"Wasn't the coffee hot?" Crash said.

Matt nodded. "Very. Huge fucking mistake," he said. His eyes watered and his face flushed red. "Goddamn."

Crash took a measured sip of her coffee. "How'd your appointment go?"

Matt wiped the tears from his eyes. "Fine."

"Want to talk about it?"

"We ever talk about it before?"

"No, but I thought—"

"Then I don't want to talk about it now."

On the walk inside, as they headed to the elevator, Matt said, "Any sign of the state police poking around?"

"Nothing so far. Should they be?"

"This isn't anything they would care about, but all the same, I prefer we keep it to ourselves."

Inside the elevator, Crash pushed the button for the fourth floor.

"No offense, Matt, but who cares?" she said. "If the staties come in, or if we catch whoever did it, what's it matter, so long as someone goes away for it?"

Once the steel doors slid shut, Matt said, "I'm tired of the state guys coming in and taking over cases. It's what they do, and they take a huge joy in it. It makes it feel like it doesn't matter what we do because they'll always be better than us."

The elevator car slowed to a stop with a gentle pulsing shimmy, and the doors opened and they exited into the hallway.

"Do you know what the sheriff's department used to do, Matt?" Crash said.

"I feel like this is where all your fancy college learning is about to come into play."

"It collected taxes. And before you say it, I know it's what we still do. But in another time, that was the sole function of sheriffs. It's why the sheriff is the villain in *Robin Hood*. That was the only law enforcement we did. It only came over time we became an investigatory agency."

Matt said nothing and instead rocked on the heels of his feet.

Crash said, "What I'm saying is, this who's-got-the-biggest-dick show with the state police, it's a waste of time. Seems like all of us working together would be the smarter way to go."

They walked side by side into Gary Campbell's room. Campbell sat up in bed watching Fox News. He looked worse than Matt expected. The old man's face was swollen and discolored, a deep purple. The swelling distorted his face, so he looked like something from a low-budget horror film where the makeup had been slapped on in a hurry. Under normal conditions Campbell would have been considered a good-looking man, well aged into his later years, but these weren't those conditions. He seemed sad and mournful, his face papered with bandages. His gray hair was tousled and scattered down his forehead. He wore rimless glasses with the right lens cracked, and he blinked large, watery eyes at the officers as they entered the room.

Matt introduced himself and Crash then explained that the sheriff's department was investigating the attack. Campbell kept his eyes on Crash, concern and wonder both on his face, as if asking himself what she was doing there.

"How are you today, Mr. Campbell?" Matt said.

"Shitty, to tell you the truth. I suppose that's what you'd expect from someone in a hospital, after something like what happened to me and Wilma."

"What have the doctors told you about your wife?"

Campbell folded his hands together. They were large and covered in age spots and fresh bruises. Matt thought they seemed fragile, like a bird's nest exposed from behind fallen leaves.

"There's swelling in her brain, and they're worried about that. She fractured her hip, broke a couple of bones." Campbell's voice cracked with emotion. "Goddamn animals in this world." He puffed out his chest. "If I'd gotten to the pistol in the bedroom, I suppose you'd have been talking about murder charges for the persons involved in this."

The broken pride of an old man was a hard thing for Matt to see. Campbell probably wanted to seem strong, able to provide, able to protect.

"I doubt that," Matt said. "Can you tell us about what happened?"

"I'm chair of my church's budget committee, and we met last night. Wilma plays piano on Sundays, so the men met downstairs, and she practiced upstairs. We got home—it must have been about ten or ten thirty. Later than I like to be driving at night, but the church is looking to expand and the meeting went long—"

"Did you notice anything suspicious when you came home?"

"Not at all. We came through the front door and—" Campbell sucked in air and reached for his chest, clutching his heart. He took a deep breath and relaxed.

"What happened when you entered the premises?" Crash said.

Campbell paused as his lips drew tight and thin against one another. "No offense, young lady, but these are details I'm not comfortable discussing in front of you."

Crash's mouth opened, but before she could say anything, Matt laid his hand on her shoulder.

"Deputy Landing is my chief deputy," Matt said. "She's an exceptional officer, and you can speak to her as you would any other deputy."

The discomfort was obvious for Campbell. Matt guessed the old man had spent most of his life sending women out of the room so men could discuss the unpleasantries of life.

Campbell nodded. "I came in first. I unlocked the door for Wilma, and as I opened it for her, someone grabbed hold of me and pulled me in and threw me into the wall. Then they took Wilma and threw her on top of me and slammed the door shut and locked it. I heard the deadbolt snap into place, and it sounded like the hammer on a gun."

"Did you see their faces?" Matt said.

"No. They were wearing masks. Rubber masks, like it was Halloween or something."

"How many were there?"

Campbell furrowed his brows. "Four. It—it happened so fast. Then, when they struck me and Wilma—"

"Did they say what they wanted?"

"No. They were animals, Sheriff. Nothing but animals." He sniffed, and a tear rolled down his cheek. "They kept beating me and Wilma and laughing about it the whole time."

"All four of them?"

"Yes."

"All of them male?"

"Yes. I guess. The masks, it was hard to tell."

"Did they seem younger? Older?"

"They sounded like they were younger, but I'm not sure. The masks muffled their voices."

"When they spoke, did they address you by name?"

He nodded. "I'm old, and I've got footprint enough in this town."

"How much of anything do you remember?"

"More than I wish I did. One of them hit Wilma upside the head, and she collapsed. She's not well, she has heart issues, and—" Campbell's voice trailed off, and he looked away to the window and the blue sky. "They dragged me to the kitchen, hitting and kicking and cursing at me. And laughing, the whole time laughing, like it was all the funniest thing ever."

Campbell pushed his face into his hand, and a soft gasping noise crept through his fingers.

Matt said, "Just a few more questions, Mr. Campbell. Do you have reason to believe they targeted you? Were they looking for something specific?"

The old man lifted his face up. "They're nothing but people who've spent their lives listening to the shit on the radio they claim is music, watching horror movies, and playing video games, and it's broken them as humans, and now they're nothing more than bottom-feeders on the rest of society." He shook his head. "We've been in that house almost forty years now, and our lives are quiet. It's Wilma and me, and I don't know what to do if—"

The unspoken words hung there for a second.

"We've contacted your daughter, Mr. Campbell," Crash said. "She said she'd—"

Campbell's face snapped into anger. "What the hell did you do that for?"

Crash and Matt exchanged looks. "We thought you—"

"Last time I checked, you weren't paid to do anyone's thinking." Campbell's tone took a sharp, angry tone. "What you should do is busy yourself finding these people and making sure they don't do this to anyone else. Good people shouldn't have to worry about this." Campbell sighed and leaned back in the bed. "Can you please go now? I'm tired, and I need to get some sleep."

Matt set a business card on the table next to Campbell's bed. "If you think of anything, please—"

Campbell closed his eyes. "You all have a good day."

***

In the hallway, free from earshot of Campbell's room, Crash said, "That was weird, right? It wasn't just a thing I'm interpreting as weird?"

"It was unusual."

"What was it about, you suppose?"

"Don't know. Don't care either unless it's got something to do with what happened last night."

"I can't remember anyone freaking out that way over mention of his kid coming to see him."

"That's between him and the kid."

"You don't have a big sense of mystery, do you, Matt?"

"Life's not about mysteries, Crash. Life's just about getting through the day to the next."

"Dark way of looking at things."

"We all can't be sunshine and puppies," Matt said as he stepped into the elevator, Crash a step behind him.

Chapter 4

Rachel sat on the back deck drinking wine when Matt got home. He watched her through the French doors that led outside from the kitchen. She held a cigarette between the fingers of one hand, and she took a drag and exhaled and used the other hand to fan away the smoke.

Matt didn't remember her smoking before their reconciliation. Maybe she had and he had been oblivious. It wouldn't have been surprising, all the hours he logged at the office, him not recognizing it. It was those hours—his mindless devotion to the job—that had led to her with the attorney, to the divorce. When he got his second chance with Rachel—Matt didn't believe in divine providence and assumed life to be a random series of happenstance and blind luck—he'd been surprised when he discovered she smoked. The lawyer had been a selfish fuck who liked women "a certain way," though, and Rachel developed the habit to stay thin, to maintain his approval.

Rachel tried to hide it from Matt, he knew. He caught her sometimes, sneaking when he wasn't around. She would toss the spent cigarette butt over the fence into the neighbor's driveway. Then she would finish her glass of wine, chew gum, spray perfume. All part of the performance.

Matt went upstairs without telling her he was home, stripped and tossed his clothes in the laundry basket, and started a warm shower. He took his time, the water washing over him, loosening the tightness in his body, reviving the tired and aching parts of himself. He ran his hands down his torso and across himself, examining the places where there had been more of him not so long ago. He imagined that he could feel himself wasting away underneath his skin, the cancer gnawing at his insides.

The bathroom door opened, the shower curtain slid open, and Rachel, naked, appeared through the steam and stepped into the tub, wrapping her arms around his waist and pulling him close to her. She kissed him. She still smelled vaguely of cigarettes, but he didn't care. He focused on the warmth of her, the water sliding between their bodies. His arms twined around her, and her breasts pressed against his chest.

"How long have you been home?" she said.

"Not long. I thought we could go to the Riverside and get dinner."

Rachel smiled. "The Riverside. You fancy devil, you. You spoil me."

Her mouth enveloped his, and they met together underneath the shower's spray until the hot water started to give out. He shut off the faucet, and she led him by the hand into the bedroom, dripping water in their wake. She pushed him gently, and he fell backward onto the bed. She climbed on top of him.

"We're soaking the sheets," he said.

"I'll wash them."

"And the mattress."

"We'll flip it."

Matt laughed. "God but I love you."

"I love you too, Matt. Now take me."

So he did.

They lay there in the aftermath of it all, their bodies wet with sweat and chilled shower water. Matt felt the cold and pulled a sheet across them, wanting it to appear he was just being considerate of her. He got cold easier now.

Rachel rolled over onto her side. Matt's head rested on the pillow, his eyes closed.

"You didn't say anything about your appointment with Dr. Fordham," she said.

"How could I? You all but raped me. I may consider pressing charges."

She flicked one of his nipples. He winced and popped an eye open and glared at her. "You're an evil woman, Rachel Simms." He closed his eyes again. "It was fine. Uneventful."

"What did he say?"

"Not much. Things are the way they are."

"That tells me nothing, Matt."

"Perhaps there's nothing to tell. Things are at a standstill."

"Cancer doesn't get to a standstill. And you are not spontaneously in remission, either. So I need you to tell me what's going on."

Matt sighed and repeated for Rachel what Fordham had told him that morning. She listened with a blank, almost stoic expression on her face as he recounted the dearth of options the doctor had given him.

"What are the odds you can move up the transplant list?"

"Don't know. Depends on if they want to give a liver to an old, out-of-shape dude like me. There could be a rich guy they decide needs it more."

"I still think we should see about me donating part of mine."

Matt shook his head. "We've had this conversation."

"No, you've had this conversation, where you make it clear you won't listen to anything I say about the matter."

"Because I'm not having you go under the knife because of me."

"Livers regenerate. I've read all about it. We have the same blood types. I don't see what the—"

Matt pushed himself up and off the bed. Standing, looking at Rachel, she seemed both smaller yet more fierce than he realized. Her eyes narrowed and her face tightened, and even naked, she seemed ready for battle.

"They'll figure this out—"

"So you say," she said.

"So I know. Trust me on this."

"Someone told me once you shouldn't ask someone to trust you, that it's a cry for forgiveness."

"That person sounds like an asshole."

"It was you."

"But a wise asshole. Very knowing. Very trustworthy, so to speak. Also, trust me when I say the Riverside is our best option for dinner tonight." He leaned down and kissed her on the forehead. "Now come on, because I want to get there before the AA crowd from St. Anthony's shows up."

Chapter 5

Matt knocked on the front door of Amy Portis's house and waited. The wheelchair ramp added onto the porch was a recent addition, he knew. Not painted or stained yet, and he wondered if he should ask if he could do that. That was what was on his mind when the front door opened.

There couldn't have been any question that Amy Portis was Carl Thompson's sister. She stood six-two barefoot, feminine with broad shoulders. She filled the door frame with a lean, sinewy body, in a Parker County Bucs T-shirt and yoga pants, mounds of curly hair spilling off her head and out into the wild. She smiled a smile full of large white teeth at the sight of Matt, and the crinkles in the corners of her eyes added to her attractiveness.

"About goddamn time you showed up," she said, hugging Matt. She stopped and pulled back and her eyes were wide and fearful. "Oh Jesus Christ, Matt, I'm sorry. I wasn't thinking. Are you okay? I didn't—"

Matt waved her words off. "I'm fine, Amy. The cancer beat you to causing the good damage already."

"Come on in," she said. She shut the door behind him and led Matt into the kitchen. "Get you a cup of coffee? Pot's fresh."

"That would be great."

Amy busied herself getting out mugs and sugar and a carton

of half-and-half.

Things were awkward between Matt and Amy after the shooting. White supremacists had shot Carl while he was protecting Rachel. The bullet penetrated his spine, left him paralyzed. The doctors told him he'd ever walk again.

Amy, protective of her brother since childhood, blamed Matt. That Carl had no reason to take a bullet this way. Why hadn't Matt been the one with Rachel? Amy didn't care about all the other pieces that had been in play that day; she only saw her brother, this mass of a man, stuck in a wheelchair for the rest of his life. It had taken Carl telling her over and over, day after day for months, before she accepted what her brother said to her: the danger was part of the job, and if he had to do it over again, he wouldn't change shit. Protecting people was what a cop did, he said.

Matt took in the surroundings. Amy's husband, Michael, was an accountant for a bottling company the next county over; the company did steady business, and the house reflected the success. The hardwood floors gleamed under the sunlight through the drawn curtains. The marble countertops were pristine. The coffeepot looked as though you would need an instruction manual the size of the Bible to operate it.

An island sat in the middle of the kitchen. There was fruit in a bowl and flowers in a vase. Matt pulled himself up onto a bench as Amy set a coffee mug in front of him. She leaned on the other side of the island, sipped from her cup.

"How are you?" she said.

"Alive, though that's liable to change."

"Rachel still love those jokes?"

"I save them for the adults-only show."

Amy sipped more coffee. "I've never understood what she was thinking, going back to you."

"You know, I'm three feet from you. I can hear what you're saying with crystal clarity."

"Drinking my coffee doesn't save you from my opinions.

You're something of a dick sometimes."

"Only sometimes?"

"I've only been around you sometimes. But you've been good to Carl since everything happened—"

"Carl and I go back to the Stone Age, Amy. What happened only happened because he was doing me a favor. Rachel and I, we won't forget that."

"Carl has always liked you. Respected you."

"Carl would have been a better sheriff than me."

Amy shook her head. "When we were kids, Mom was forever having to send him back to neighbors' houses to apologize for being too rough, or mouthing off and saying something he should have thought twice about saying. But he'd listen to you. Hell if I ever understood why."

"The obvious answer is the quiet sense of power and authority I exude." Matt looked toward the back door. "He outside?"

"Yeah."

Since Carl's return from Pittsburgh and his first rounds of intensive physical therapy, and after moving into his sister's house, Matt knew he spent much of his time on the back porch. Whenever Matt came over, Carl was out there reading, tapping away on his iPad, or staring out over the yard.

"At least it's fresh air, I suppose," Matt said.

"He says he's done with physical therapy. Says there's no reason to keep going. He's down more. More defeated. He's not eating much. He's always either out there or in his room."

"He seemed fine when I've talked to him."

"You're here a few hours a week, Matt. I live with him. I'm the one who has to help hoist him in and out of the bathtub and has to empty a colostomy bag. I'll do it so long as I can, because he's my brother and I love him, but no one thinks they'll have to dump their brother's shit and piss out of a bag, either. Nothing prepares you for that. He was my hero growing up, and now I have to hide I want to puke every time. He's ashamed of something that isn't even his fucking fault." She sucked in air through her teeth and seemed to let herself catch her words before saying anything else.

Matt reached across the table and laid his hand on hers. It sat there for a moment before she turned it over and wrapped her fingers around his hand and squeezed. At first, it seemed a kind, simple embrace. Then it grew tighter and tighter, and Matt winced in pain. He saw a smile on Amy's face and he pulled away, and she let him go. He shook his hand, moving blood through it.

"You're a goddamn piece of work, Amy," he said.

"Yeah, I'm a bitter and spiteful cunt." She took her coffee cup and headed out of the kitchen. "Go talk to Carl. I've got shit to do."

The back deck of the house overlooked several acres of un-fenced land. The stretch of land offered a spectacular view of the sunrise. Matt remembered the weekend he and Carl had spent with Michael, Amy's husband, building the deck, drinking beer, and cursing and laughing. It hadn't been long after Rachel left him, and Matt had needed something to keep him busy, to keep his mind off of other things. Carl had all but dragged him over, and he had protested going the entire time, but once they started swinging hammers and sweating, he had enjoyed himself.

When they had finished, Michael cooked steaks on the grill, and Carl and Matt kept on drinking, and they ended up with Amy driving them both home, and the next morning a deputy—Matt couldn't remember who—drove them back out to pick up their cars. They were both hung-over, masked in hang-dog expressions of veiled regret, wearing sunglasses though only the faintest hint of sun peeked out. It was one of the best times Matt could remember from that period, when there hadn't seemed to be too many good times.

This morning, a thin, low-lying fog hung in the air. It made seeing into the distance of the property almost impossible, but

Matt thought he saw the silhouette of a deer about a hundred feet away.

Carl was at the edge of the deck, watching the silhouette. Even in his wheelchair, Carl seemed a huge man. He was six-four, and he had been built like a linebacker back in the day. He had lost some of that weight, and the muscle with it, but in the wheelchair, he still carried himself like a brute-even if hunched over, a weakened version of his self.

Matt knew from his days hunting that the most dangerous animal was a wounded one.

Carl had let his hair grow out, so it hung shaggy over his ears, down his neck. He had a beard now, a bushy growth ready to swallow his face whole. He wore a polo shirt and clutched a coffee cup in his lap. Matt stepped up beside him. Carl kept his attention focused on the silhouette in the backyard.

"How long has he been there?" Matt said.

"Most of the morning. There's a family that comes out. This one, he's younger. You look hard enough, you can see the nubs working their way out on the top of his head." Carl sipped his coffee. "He'll be a fucking beast."

"They get close?"

"Only at night. I can see 'em from my bedroom. They'll come up and eat Amy's flowers, or on the little box garden she keeps trying to grow."

"I admire your sister's persistence in killing vegetation."

"You work with the gifts God grants you. It's like she's the living embodiment of one of those Old Testament plagues sent to wipe out the crops. I suppose we're lucky she can't make it rain frogs."

"It would make driving to work difficult. I don't know how my windshield wipers would handle it."

"The squishing noise would be the worst part."

Matt gagged.

Carl laughed. "Pussy."

Matt dragged a patio chair next to Carl and sat down.

Carl looked at him. "Tired?"

"If I stand for too long."

"Pardon me if I'm jealous of the standing."

"It's overrated."

"I'll take your word on it."

"Always a mistake."

"So I've learned. How you doing otherwise?"

"I'm dying. Outside that, I'm great."

"I hear dying puts a big crimp on plans."

"You stop buying green bananas." Matt drank his coffee. "I realized the other day I'm not sure what to do about my vacation time next year. I'd toyed with taking Rachel and going up to the Poconos, but then I thought, 'Fuck, I don't want to put a deposit down on a cabin and make the arrangements, and then, you know, be dead before we can go.' It seems like something inconsiderate to leave Rachel with."

"Maybe the Poconos would be the best thing for her. Take her mind off things."

"So it's a win-win situation, is what you're saying."

"For Rachel. Less so for you. Mind you, I'm still single, so maybe she and I could go together."

"That's generous of you."

"I'm always looking out for you."

"What would I do without you?"

"I hope you never have to know."

"And besides that, you're the second person to offer to console Rachel in her time of grief after I'm dead."

"Because we all know you swung outside your weight class with her."

"I can't argue that with you. What about you? Where's your head been at?"

"Attached to my neck, like it tends to be."

"Amy says you're not going to physical therapy anymore."

"Yeah, I don't see where that'll do me any good. I ain't

walking anytime soon, so I figure fuck that noise."

Matt looked at Carl. He was still broad in the chest, with thick forearms and developed biceps from using the free weights in the spare bedroom. Carl was too prideful to let himself shrivel away. He looked solid and well-constructed, if a smaller version than before.

"What about the shrink?" Matt said.

"What about her?"

"You still going?"

"I am."

"That helping?"

"I go in twice a week and talk. She asks me how I'm feeling. I tell her I'm angry, I'm frustrated, I consider eating the barrel of a pistol, and then I get the fuck over myself and go push weights until whatever's left I can feel, until that hurts. This is my cycle almost every goddamn day, and until I figure out how to stand up and walk out of this chair, it's unlikely to change."

"What's she tell you?"

"That what I'm feeling is normal, and that I need to accept this as my new normal."

"I know you well enough that that won't happen."

"Fuck no it won't. I'm just not sure how long I can keep being angry and staring at deer."

"You could come back to work."

"No, I could roll back into the office and shuffle papers around and pretend anything I did mattered."

"You should talk to Henry Malone. His experience, it's not too dissimilar."

"We talked."

"How was that?"

"Once he got past being glib and trying to be funny, it was okay." Carl shrugged. "Big difference between him and me, though, is he walked in, and he walked out. He got shot, all it did was take out his knee. I got shot, and I can't feel anything from the waist down. So while maybe you think the stories are the same, they're not. We won't be brothers in arms like that."

"I don't know. Think it over. You're both colossal pains in the ass."

They went back inside. Amy was cooking bacon and eggs, and she asked Matt if he wanted any.

"I can't. I need to get to the office."

Carl said, "You on that home invasion?"

"Yeah. Nasty stuff."

"How's it coming?"

"Nothing so far. Crash is looking into things."

"She adjusting to being a big shot now?"

"She's doing fine, though every time I look at her, it feels like I should remind her she's late for fifth-period algebra. Combine that with people treating her like it's the eighteenth century and they feel the need to tell you it's weird to have a woman as your chief deputy. They act like she's a delicate flower."

"Have you mentioned to these people that Crash has a mouth that would shame a sailor?"

"I'll point that out to them next time." Matt ran his hand over his face, eyeing Carl's. "This thing. How long you plan on keeping that happening?"

Carl brushed the back of his hand over his beard. "I'm going for the 'crippled lumberjack' look. I hear it's a thing."

Matt's eyes flashed over in Amy's direction. She had her back to the men, but he watched her shoulders tighten and hunch at Carl's words, then struggle to relax.

The new normal.

Chapter 6

Matt was in his office drinking coffee when Crash knocked on the door and walked in before he could say anything.

Matt glanced up from his laptop, drugstore cheaters on the end of his nose.

"Crash?" he said.

Crash paused where she was. "Yes, Matt?"

"Aren't you supposed to wait for someone to tell you to come in?"

"Would you prefer I close the door and we do this all over again?"

"Not really, and not my point anyway. It's just there are codes of decorum in a polite society."

"My parents did a good job of imparting those things on me."

"I'd quibble with that since you didn't give me a chance to say 'Come on in' after you'd knocked. Who knows what I could have been doing in here."

"What were you doing?"

"Drinking coffee and typing reports."

"Nothing scandalous."

"Nothing that would get me on the front page of the newspaper."

"Then I'm not sure what this conversation is all about."

Matt removed his glasses. "What do you want, Crash?"

"Iris Campbell—Gary Campbell's daughter—she's here."

"Show her on in."

"Should I knock first?"

"Just let her in."

Iris Campbell was dressed in slim-cut jeans and a paper-thin cardigan sweater over a T-shirt. She moved in long strides, graceful in high-heeled boots, until she reached the other side of Matt's desk. She looked to be somewhere in her well-preserved forties, tan, thin-lipped with a narrow nose that divided her face into near-symmetrical halves. Her brown eyes peered through thin slits, and her brown hair reached past her shoulders.

Matt stood and reached out a hand. She looked at it, then back up at him. Matt glanced at his hand, flipping it back and forth, and drew it back. He shrugged and gestured to his visitor's chair.

"Have a seat, Ms. Campbell?" he said.

"It's 'Warner,'" she said, folding her arms across her chest. "How's my mother?"

"The hospital could answer that question better than I can. Are you planning on sitting down, Ms. Warner, because if we're being honest here, I need to."

Her face remained blank, yet fierce. "I'm not stopping you."

Matt sat back in his chair. "Would you like a cup of coffee? Water? Someone to dislodge the branch shoved up your ass?"

She arched an eyebrow. A hint of a smile flickered in the corner of her mouth. "Is this how you talk to everyone, Sheriff?"

"My manners are terrible, but they're what they are. Think of those without any manners at all, how lonely they must feel."

She sat down. Matt glanced up at Crash, still standing beside the open door.

"We're good," Matt said. "Thanks for showing Ms. Warner in."

Crash nodded and drew Matt's office door shut until the catch clicked.

Matt smiled at her from across the desk. "Have you been to

the hospital?"

"Not yet. I'm waiting until there's something definitive about my mother."

"What about your father?"

She smiled this time, but it was the smile of a cat with a mouse caught underneath its paw. "I'm rooting for the old man to contract MRSA." She produced a pack of cigarettes from her purse and shook a stick loose.

"You can't smoke in here," Matt said. "County rules."

"Since when?"

"Since the board of health banned smoking in restaurants. Such as restaurants that Parker County has. Then the county commission nixed it in public buildings."

She tossed everything back into her purse. "Crying shame, the things the government takes from you."

"I'm sure there'll be plenty of time for lung cancer."

"I don't need your judgmental attitude, Sheriff. There's enough in my life without civil servants feeling the need to lecture me on my bad habits."

"The smoking was the only one I know about, but hang around a while and I'll see what I can say about your posture or if you bite your nails."

"I don't like your tone, Sheriff. Are you one of those people who thinks they're funny when they're not?"

"I'm self-entertaining. Should I presume you are estranged from your father?"

"Happily so."

"Any reason?"

"Many, though I doubt they're any of your business. I left Parker County the day after I graduated high school, and I've made sure not to look back ever since. I keep in contact with my mother, trying to encourage her to leave that miserable bastard. None of my heeds have taken root."

"What do you do, Ms. Warner?"

"I'm a freelance writer, based out of Cincinnati. It isn't a glamorous life, but it pays my bills and means I'm not beholden to him or my mother."

"'Him' meaning your father?"

"Yes."

"Is your father rich?"

"My father's accumulated money over the years. I don't know how you're categorizing *rich* these days."

"He's not in a house I'd associate with a rich man."

"There are two ways for a man to become rich: one is by making a lot of money, and the other is not to spend any of said money. My father practiced both techniques throughout his life."

"But you're still close to your mother?"

"We speak. He doesn't know. He'll flip his shit when he finds out."

"Spoiler alert: he already has."

"Oh joy." She rolled her eyes. "You told him?"

"Guilty."

"Goddammit." She spit the words out. "Sheriff, with all due offense, you should just keep your nose out of the business of others."

"It's what I do. We all have to play to our gifts, Ms. Warner."

"Call me Iris. Warner is a pen name. The one act of decency my father ever committed, when I was growing up, he let me watch old movies with him, and I loved the old Warner Bros. films. Bogart and Cagney and all the tough guys." Iris cast an eye across the desk at Matt, a look of evaluation, sizing him up. "Are you a tough guy, Sheriff?"

"I'm practically bulletproof, Iris," he said. "Any idea why someone would attack your parents?"

"I'm sure my father's given people plenty of reasons, but I'm not sure on specifics if that's what you're asking." She folded her hands together and rested her elbows on her knees. "My mother's a good woman, though. A good person, gender be damned. I don't understand her blind devotion to my father, but she is who she is. I need to know you'll catch the people who did this to her."

"My department will do everything it can to catch these men, Iris. You have my word."

"How much is your word worth, Sheriff?"

"I suppose that depends on who's asking."

Iris stood up. Matt took a beat to appreciate the movement. "I'm going to go to the hospital," she said and took a business card from her purse, set it on Matt's desk. Matt reached into a drawer and handed Iris one of his own cards. He tried to give out as many as he could; since the cancer, he joked he didn't know how long they would still be good.

Iris dropped the card into her purse. "If you find out anything, please let me know, Sheriff. I'll be in town for a while."

Matt walked Iris Warner to the door. "Thanks for stopping by, Ms. Warner."

He watched her walk to the elevator. She passed Crash through the metal doors as he exited and she entered. Crash walked into the office.

"She's something else, isn't she?" she said.

"People are almost invariably something else, Crash. The question is always what those things are."

Chapter 7

Gloria Miller offered Matt coffee as she led him into the living room. He declined. Gloria's double-wide was small but well kept, the air thick with a mixture of cigarette smoke and scented candles. Worn couch cushions threatened to expose the stuffing within. A half-empty coffee cup rested next to a half-smoked cigarette in an ashtray, which was next to a copy of one of those celebrity magazines about pretty people and their lives so many miles away.

"I'm sorry about how the place looks," Gloria said as they sat down, Gloria on the couch and Matt in a chair at her side. She sipped at her coffee. "There's just so many hours in the day, and—"

Matt reached out and touched her arm. "It's fine, Gloria. Why don't we relax here and talk, okay?"

Gloria smiled but still seemed embarrassed. She looked the epitome of a farmer's wife. A big-boned woman with a ruddy face and broad shoulders, dressed in a thin hoodie and blue jeans, with board-straight dark hair streaked with gray. Matt felt like he could put Gloria's high school senior photo next to her that day and, other than the gray, she looked about the same as she had for the twenty-five-plus years he had known her.

She took a deep breath, and it was a stuttering sound, a struggle to get the air into her lungs. Her eyes seemed tired, as though she hadn't known sleep in days.

"Micki's gone," she said.

"Your daughter Micki?"

She nodded. "Michelle, but no one's called her that since she was little." Gloria twisted her hands together. "She's seventeen. It's not like she's a bad kid, Matt, but she makes some bad choices."

"That's what they do, Gloria. They're nothing but bad ideas and pushing boundaries. It's why they call 'em *teenagers*. How long has she been missing?"

"Three days. Please don't think I'm a bad mom. It's just me and her and her brothers, and I work double shifts at the plant—"

"No judgments, Gloria." He let his tone shift and his voice lighten so he could sound calming and soothing. He knew the routine, the approach to take in these circumstances. Kids, they disappeared all the time. Take off for a few days. More often than not, they showed up, metaphorical hat in hand, an understanding they had fucked up. Matt chalked it all up to rebellious streaks, something the kid needed to work out.

"What happened?" he said.

"Nothing. I mean, nothing more than usual. Me and her, we butt heads. She's home with the boys more than she likes; she wants to have her a life, and I understand, but the boys, I can't leave them by themselves, and it's been hard since their dad left."

"Three days ago would put it at Saturday, right?"

"Yes. I had an early shift, and then they needed me to take overtime, and I couldn't say no to it, and when I got home, she wasn't here."

"You still over at the cookie factory?"

Gloria nodded. "Five, six days a week for almost fifteen years."

"Your sons, did they say anything about when she left?"

"Alex said Micki got a phone call about four. She took the phone into her room and talked, and she came out with a bag and said she'd be gone for a while. I got home after six, and they were both sitting there staring at the TV, playing video games. I was pissed as hell because I had asked her to start dinner, and the boys hadn't had lunch or anything."

"Does Micki have a cell phone?"

Gloria laughed. "Hell no, and don't think for a minute she's done anything but whine about that. But I don't have that kind of money, Matt."

"So the call came in on your land-line?"

"Yes."

"Did you check the caller ID?"

"I did and called the number back, and all it did was ring and ring."

"You remember the number?"

"Better than that." She fished into her purse, bringing things out and setting them on her lap: a shabby and cheap-looking wallet, a small makeup bag, loose tissues, a crumpled pack of cigarettes, gum. She dug until she drew out a folded sheet of paper to give to Matt. Matt looked at the number and set the paper on the coffee table.

"What about her friends? Have you talked to them? Or her girlfriends?"

"I don't know who Micki hangs out with. I'm at work so much—" Gloria's cheeks flushed, her eyes rimmed with red.

"We'll go by the school. Her teachers will know who she's friends with."

She wiped away the tears, streaking her makeup until black lines ran up from the corner of each eye. "I'm so embarrassed. We don't have much, and I know we're one of those families people look at and they're ashamed for us, but I do the best I can with what I've got."

"No one thinks anything like that about you, Gloria."

"It's sweet of you to lie, Matt, but I live in this town, and the people here, they're how they are. I've talked shit about folks with less than me because that's what we do."

Matt called Crash on his cell phone. Gave her the number

and asked her to run it down. Crash said sure, took down the number, and hung up.

Matt returned his phone to his pocket. "I'll need a picture of Micki? Something we can pass around to the deputies."

Gloria went back into her purse and brought out an envelope and handed it to Matt. "I had to go back to the drug-store and print these out. You know, no one has real pictures anymore; everything's digital and on your phone these days."

Matt pulled out the top photo from the envelope. Micki Miller had the look of a teenager who rebelled by looking like every other teenager who rebelled, with long hair dyed black, unbrushed, and matted into knots. She lined her eyes with thick black makeup, and her lips were a vivid red, her skin the color of paper. She was still round on the edges, though, without those hard pieces that kids got from working so hard to grow up too fast. Micki Miller looked like a teenager, and she battled against it with everything in her. Her AC/DC T-shirt was frayed and faded, a thrift store buy and not an overpriced vintage reproduction, and she wore a scowl in obvious distaste at having her picture taken.

Matt slid the photo back in and set the envelope aside. He laid his hand on Gloria's shoulder.

"She's a kid. We'll find her hiding out with friends somewhere, I can almost guarantee."

Gloria looked down at Matt's hand and tried to smile, but there wasn't much behind it. She wasn't a woman who could afford to muster too much hope.

"People saying you're sick," she said. "That true?"

Matt brought back his hand. "How did you hear?"

"Red Raymond was talking about it on break. Said he'd heard from someone else. They're saying it's cancer."

"It is."

"What kind?"

"Liver."

Gloria sniffed and wiped at her nose with the back of her

hand. "Damn but I'm sorry, Matt. How bad is it?"

"You ever known any cancer that's good?"

"Don't suppose I have."

"I'm gonna be fine. Looking at options. I'll be around a while. Been alive this long, I don't see a good reason to stop yet."

Matt and Gloria stood, and Gloria patted Matt on the shoulder. "That's good to know. I always liked you."

Matt smiled. "You're an excellent judge of character then, Gloria."

Chapter 8

Crash knocked on Matt's office door. Matt called out, "Enter!"
Crash walked in and set a manila folder on the desk.
Matt glanced at it, then to Crash.
"That the report on the telephone number?" Matt said.
"It is."
"It looks formal. You put it in a folder and everything."
"Presentation counts."
"If you're in a cooking competition, yes." He flipped the folder open and thumbed through the pages. "Are you going to make me read this thing, or can you save me the trouble and tell me what I need to know?"
"The number goes to a pay-as-you-go cell phone you pick up at Walmart. Purchased with cash two months ago. The account's been re-upped a few times through cards you buy for that provider."
"Cards also paid for with cash, I would suppose."
"Yes, sir."
Matt tipped his glasses to the end of his nose. "Did you call me *sir*?"
"I did."
"Stop that shit. Makes me sound old."
"If we want to pick at nits, you're older than I am. And you are the sheriff. I thought I'd try out a new level of respecting authority."

"Are you working to be a pain in the ass today?"

"Somewhat. How's it working?"

"Like a charm."

Crash sat down in the visitor's chair. Matt nodded and went back to the folder's contents.

"Please, make yourself comfortable."

Crash crossed her legs, right leg at the left knee, and rested her forearms on the chair arms.

"What was the deal with Mrs. Miller's husband?" she said.

Matt looked up from the report.

"How do you know about her husband?" he said.

"I might have looked up the entire family after you called."

Matt nodded. "His name was Tyson Miller. He and Gloria got married out of high school. Gloria was raised in one of those churches where the women aren't supposed to cut their hair, and they wear denim skirts to the knees. She rebelled against her parents by marrying Tyson. The Millers, they're a family with weight."

"Money?"

"A different weight. It's the kind you get from a pit bull on logging chains in the front yard, and kids get warned not to trick-or-trick at your house, and you've got cars on blocks, but there's no VINs or registration, so even though you know they stole the cars, you can't prove it."

"They're thugs."

"The term *thug* implies intelligence and organization the Millers don't have. The whole family'll spend a day working to scam a dollar when they could have worked a real job and made ten bucks. They'll sell you whatever prescription they get, be it OxyContin or antibiotics. Two of 'em died from electrocution while stealing copper wire, the second one buying it four months after the first one, because the first one dying didn't teach them anything."

"They sound like slow learners."

"Closer to no learners, but they're persistent, which I guess counts for something. Gloria married Tyson and from what I understand, things were okay the first few years. Gloria miscarried before her daughter came around, and she worked to keep things together while Tyson focused on doing what Millers do, which was as little as possible. He'd get busted on some minor shit—dealing pot or selling stolen tools from the car parts store—but nothing enough to hang him, and besides, he had a wife and kids, and he wasn't what anyone would have called a menace except to himself. He was smart enough to keep out of the worst of things and stupid enough to keep landing in annoying shit."

"She said he's gone, though. He doing time somewhere?"

"Nothing simple like that. He just disappeared. Damndest thing. The little girl couldn't have been much more than a year or two old. Hell, the post office probably has his missing persons posters hanging on the wall still. Gloria called up and said he had left one morning and never came home. Like the earth sucked him underneath."

"Weird."

"I suppose. He was nothing but a crook, but there wasn't anything that said Tyson would have walked out on 'em that way. No real historical precedent for a Miller leaving Parker County, either. But it stuck Gloria raising her daughter, and then she had the twins on accident a few years ago. Far as I know, she's been working double shifts at that factory, trying to make the ends meet."

"Awful lot of work raising kids by yourself. Can't imagine his family's got much to contribute."

"They're as useful as tits on a boar hog. Gloria's like the rest of us, working out of our leagues and overcompensating for the shortcomings."

"It sounds like seeing a shrink has paid off for you."

"I took up meditation too. Someone recommended it for the cancer."

"Is it working?"

"I still have cancer, so no, but I'm not as worried about it, so yes."

"I realized the other day, Steve Jobs had liver cancer too, didn't he?"

"He did."

Crash waited a beat.

"He died from it."

Matt nodded. "He did."

Another beat.

"I'm sorry, Matt."

"Why? I didn't know Steve Jobs."

Crash smiled. It was a painful expression.

Matt came out of his chair and around the desk, leaning his ass against it. "Go by the high school in the morning and talk to the principal. See if there's anyone from Micki Miller's classes she was friends with. I can almost promise you that cell phone number belongs to a boy."

"Or a girl. High school kids, they don't give a fuck these days."

"I have the same amount of fucks to give, but regardless, the number goes to someone Micki's involved with, and if we find that person, we find out where she is."

"What about the Campbell home invasion?"

"What about it? Please tell me the neighbors saw something."

"We checked up and down the street and no one said they saw anything."

"To be expected. Any word on Mrs. Campbell?"

"Nothing new. She's still unconscious. They're trying to keep the brain swelling down, but there are other medical issues at play. She's an old woman. None of it sounds good."

"If that happens, this becomes a homicide case."

"That might be enough to make the state police come in."

"Fuck but I hope not. Last thing I need in my life is Jackie Hall showing up at my door."

"He's that lieutenant you don't like, right?"

"He is."

"Why don't you like him?"

"Because he doesn't like me."

"Then why doesn't he like you?"

"It's got something to do with me not liking him."

"This sounds extremely cyclical."

"Round and round the world spins, I guess."

Crash rose to her feet. "Might not be the worst thing, having the state investigate. Would be one less worry on our heads."

"Would be, but I'd rather it not happen if we can make that so."

"This is nothing but a matter of pride for you, isn't it?"

"I'm a guy, Crash. Pride keeps us going most days."

She shook her head. "You all never stop being little boys, do you?"

"We do not; we just keep wanting bigger toys."

Chapter 9

The Campbell house looked more inviting in the daylight, the sun casting off the shadows and lighting the house like a painting hung in a church vestibule. Matt knew that through the darkness, under whirling police car lights, anywhere could seem sinister.

Matt knocked on the front door and hooked his thumbs into the top of his pants, resting his hands over his gun belt. He had opted to wear a full uniform today, to seem more official. It didn't fit well, and he had studied himself in the mirror before leaving the house this morning. He felt like a child playing dress up, wearing his big brother's hand-me-downs. The top button was fastened, and he wore the black tie with it, but the collar was too large and hung loose, and it made him seem even smaller and thinner than he was.

He heard movement from inside, a man's voice muttering, and the rhythmic thuds of a cane landing against the floor. The big wooden door creaked on its hinges, and Gary Campbell stared at Matt through the screen door. His face was still splashed with purple bruises, but they had changed to a mustard-like yellow, blending with a mixture of age spots. Campbell narrowed his eyes behind large rimless glasses as he pursed his lips together.

"Sheriff," Campbell said.

"Mr. Campbell. How are you feeling?"

"I'm fine, all things supposed. What can I do for you?"

"If you're up for it, I'd like to talk to you a little more about the attack the other night."

Campbell shook his head. "Talked to you at the hospital. Talked to your deputies. I'm well and done talking. You should be out there catching these people."

"I'm just asking for five minutes of your time, to see if there's anything else from that night."

The old man sighed. It was a painful, raspy sound that broke down into a rattling cough. Campbell raised a hand and braced himself against the inside wall until the coughing subsided. He looked up at Matt with swollen, watery eyes that seemed on the verge of popping free from his head, and he opened the door.

Campbell led Matt into the living room and dropped into a recliner. His body slumped over, and he seemed to resemble a hedgehog curling into a protective ball.

Campbell motioned to the love seat. "Sit your ass down if you insist on this."

Matt lowered himself onto the sofa. He guessed the furniture had been expensive when purchased decades ago, with loud patterns and low, arched backs and drapes hanging to the floor. Now, the room, and its contents—Campbell included—seemed like a museum display, uncomfortable from years of use, worn out and tired and ready to be put away one last time.

Like Campbell, Matt thought. *Like me.*

On the end table next to Campbell's chair were three separate compartmentalized pill containers, each lid marked for a different day. Campbell popped the lid on one and dumped the contents—several pills of varying shapes and sizes and colors, looking like mints or candy—and threw them into his mouth. He swallowed, struggling at first, then reached for the glass of water and took a long drink to force them down. He heaved a deep breath and exhaled.

"I'll offer you a bit of free advice, Sheriff," Campbell said. "Don't get old. You're captive to an endless series of medications and humiliating medical procedures. If society had a drop of decency, we'd plop old goats like me on icebergs and let us float off into our great beyonds."

Matt leaned back in the love seat, trying to get himself comfortable but not able to. "Doesn't sound like an appealing way to spend the twilight years." He shifted his weight around, working to get his bones in spots where cushion springs didn't push up against them.

Campbell noticed Matt's movements and laughed. "My wife won't let me get rid of that damn chair. She says we're old, and we're the only ones here, so why go to the expense of dealing with new furniture."

"For your own comfort, I suppose."

"No one ever sits on that thing. You're the first person in years." Campbell smiled. "What do you want, Sheriff? I need to take a nap soon before I go to the hospital and visit Wilma."

"How's she doing?"

"She's unconscious still. Doctors won't know anything until she wakes up, so all I can do is sit around and wait."

"I'm very sorry, Mr. Campbell."

"Don't apologize; a man in authority doesn't apologize for things. He acts. Do your goddamn job and catch these people."

Matt brought out a notepad and a pen from his shirt pocket. "That's why I'm here. I wanted to see if you might remember anything additional from the attack."

"I remember what I told you, Sheriff. I never got a look at either of them. They were both wearing masks."

Matt paused, pen over the notepad. He flipped through a few pages. "Both?"

Campbell frowned. "What did I say?"

"You say 'both.' So there were two attackers? Because you said at the hospital that there were four."

Campbell blinked several times and ran a hand over his liver-spotted skull. There were still bandages and bruises.

"I mean *all*, not both. Sorry."

"Right, but just before that, you said 'either of them,' so that sounds like you saw two people."

"Sheriff, I'm an old man who got brained upside the head. Are you going to sit there and try to call me out on something because I might have gotten words mixed up?"

"Not at all, Mr. Campbell. But I need to know for sure what you saw that night."

"I saw four people. I presume they were men. Like I said before, they wore masks, so I couldn't tell, but their voices were husky. They might have been older. I'm not sure about that, either. Probably because they beat me like a dog."

"And you're sure they came in through the back door?"

"Yes. I had to have a new door installed this morning, and the locksmith came by and keyed a new lock for me. I don't trust the locks that come with those doors, anyway."

"Did the men say they wanted anything? Money? Jewelry? Was anything stolen?"

"No. I've not found anything missing, not that I've had much chance to look."

"Would you recognize their voices if you heard them again?"

"Doubtful."

"What about clothing? What were they wearing?"

"Blue jeans. T-shirts. The way kids dress these days."

"But you think they were older?"

"Yes. I—" Campbell's head dropped. "I can't be sure, Sheriff. I'm sorry."

Matt put the pen and notepad away. "That's fine, Mr. Campbell. I won't take up any more of your time." He stood and watched as Campbell worked to do the same. "Stay where you are, sir. I can show myself out."

Campbell fell back into the chair with a grateful sigh. "I appreciate that, Sheriff."

"Are you able to drive yourself to the hospital? Or will your daughter be coming by to pick you up?"

Campbell's body stiffened and his face dropped into something expressionless. "My daughter's no concern of yours, Sheriff. I'd appreciate it if you'd just choose not to bring her up." He pulled back on a lever on the chair's side, reclining the chair as he closed his eyes. "I need that nap now, if it's all the same to you, Sheriff."

Matt surveyed the room, the pall of sadness that lay over everything like a wet blanket heavy and smothering. This was what aging bought you: a contemptuous despair, a waiting for finality. This phase in life played like the last minutes of a movie, where you waited for the closing credits to appear. To Matt, aging seemed like a luxury he didn't have, and he wasn't sure if this was the price he wanted to pay for the extra time. It might be considered unfair and cruel that this was the reward someone got at the end of their life.

Near the television, Matt noticed the photographs clustered together in tarnished brass frames, the pictures themselves aging and yellowing from time. He recognized them as pictures of a younger version of Campbell, grouped with other men at different social events. The images showed a sharp passage of time, with the clothing changing from polyester pants and wide colors in the seventies to pastel polo shirts and khakis by what Matt guessed was the late nineties. Hair got long, got short, then vanished.

Matt said, "When were these photos taken?"

Campbell's eyes opened, and he craned his head up at Matt. "Long time ago, Sheriff. A long, long time ago." Campbell's voice lightened, a tone that denoted pleasant memories. "That was the local chapter of the Benevolent Order of the Everlasting Knights."

"I'm not familiar with them."

"You wouldn't be; fraternal groups like that aren't for young men like yourself the way they were for the men of my generation. When I owned the stores, it was a common thing to join, and you worked with the community. That way, you got to know the people who did business in town, and you gave back to your customers."

Matt tapped at the glass of one photo. It was a prime seventies shot, full of thick muttonchop sideburns and paisley shirts and nut-hugger shorts and everyone holding a cigarette and a can of beer. "I'd guess you were all a rather social bunch."

"Everyone's young once, Sheriff. It's all on credit, where you have your good times then, and you pay for it all years down the road. Now if you don't mind—"

Matt took his cue. "You have a good day, Mr. Campbell."

Outside, Matt pulled the door shut, listening for the click, and gave the doorknob a twist to make sure the lock had caught. He headed back toward his cruiser parked in the driveway. Walking down the sidewalk, he glanced toward the shrubs planted against the house, where the cabling bolted into the house exterior caught his eye. He looked up, following the cable's path, until he saw the video camera mounted underneath an overhang.

Matt walked around the house perimeter and found two more cameras—one directed toward the back door, and another at the garage.

Chapter 10

Nothing about Dr. Lillian Wilder screamed "high school principal," which worked to Wilder's advantage, Crash thought. She was younger than Crash remembered her own principals or teachers being, though Crash knew she herself wasn't so far outside the high school experience. Crash had expected someone older, someone befitting the *doctor* part of her name. Instead, what she got was a smiling woman, about forty, with well-styled blonde hair, wearing a smart red dress and chunky black heels and thin-framed black glasses.

Wilder pulled Micki's class schedule from her computer and printed out two copies—one for herself and one for Crash—before leading Crash out of her office.

"Some of Michelle's teachers have been asking about her," Wilder said as she guided Crash through the school corridors. The hallway was still. The only sound as they passed by classroom doors were teachers working their way through practiced rituals. The silhouettes of students moved behind the frosted glass: some remained straight and alert, others stared away into the void, and others struggled not to topple over asleep.

"Micki's teachers ever say they've had problems with her?"

"No. She's never been a disciplinary issue. Then again, we have more than a thousand students, so to get attention in the front office, you're either a star or a problem. The very top and the very bottom get the most attention; the rest get left to their own devices."

Wilder stopped outside a room and double-checked the printout. "This is Michelle's—Micki's—this is her second-period English. The instructor is Mr. Fitzgerald."

Wilder knocked on the door. A man's voice on the other side said, "Come in," and Wilder opened the door.

Mr. Fitzgerald was older, bald, round around the middle, and wore shiny gray slacks with a permanent crease, a short-sleeved dress shirt, and a tie that hung too short with a thick knot tight at the throat. Scrawled on the dry erase board behind him were character names and concept themes from Faulkner's *The Sound and the Fury*. The students stared at him with a mixture of boredom and thinly veiled contempt.

The students turned to Wilder and Crash standing in the doorway, most of them looking grateful for the reprieve. When they saw Crash in her uniform, a low buzz began and spread across the room like a poisonous cloud.

Fitzgerald smiled at them. Wilder motioned for him.

"Could we have a moment, Mr. Fitzgerald?" she said.

Fitzgerald told the students to read ahead and walked into the hallway and shut the door.

He assessed Crash with suspicion and curiosity behind thick-lensed glasses. "I'm guessing this isn't about those speeding tickets, is it?"

Wilder gave a small, half-hearted laugh, the sound Fitzgerald might have expected. "Chief Deputy Landing is here about Michelle Miller. A student in your class."

Fitzgerald nodded. "Micki. She has been MIA for a while now."

Crash removed her hat. "Micki's mother filed a missing-persons report. We thought some of her friends might have information that would help."

Fitzgerald pursed his lips, tented his fingers together. "Micki's usually quiet in class. My class, at least. She's smart. Puts effort into her work. Keeps to herself." His eyes trailed toward the door, and he leaned toward the glass, listening. "There's not very many people she talks to regularly. Your best bet might be Cassie Peters; she sits across from her. They're chatty together."

He poked his head inside and called Cassie out to join them.

Cassie Peters was tiny and red-haired, pale-skinned, with dark eye makeup and blood-red lipstick. She wore a Misfits T-shirt and skinny jeans ripped strategically in spots. She kept her arms crossed against her torso and her back against a wall of lockers as her eyes flitted between faces.

"Am I in trouble?" she said. "Because—"

"There's no trouble, Cassie," Wilder said. "But we are worried about Micki Miller, and Mr. Fitzgerald said you're friends with her. That true?"

Cassie's body loosened until she was almost holding herself up against the wall, and she shrugged. "We talk, but we don't hang, anything like that." The look of casual disregard vanished from her face. For a moment, she gave up that practiced teenage sense of not caring and seemed concerned. "Is she okay?"

Crash said, "That's what we're trying to find out. Her mother hasn't seen her in several days, and she can't get in touch with her. She's worried."

And just like that, Cassie turned back on the attitude. Eyes went hard. A slight smirk curled on the edge of her mouth. "She's fine. Her mother, she doesn't give a shit about her except for dealing with her asshole brothers."

Fitzgerald tapped Cassie's shoulder with a sharp poke. "Cassie, watch your mouth." His voice was sharp and practiced. "That language isn't tolerated here."

Wilder set one hand on the teacher's shoulder. "Why don't you go back to class and let the deputy and me talk to Cassie?"

Fitzgerald nodded an acquiescence and walked back into the classroom.

"Okay, class, enough excitement for the day," he said as he closed the door behind him. "Back to Faulkner."

Wilder stepped in closer to Cassie, leaning forward over her, and said, "Cassie, you can turn off the hard-ass attitude now. If Micki has gone somewhere and you know where she is, you need to tell us." Her voice took on an edge, and Cassie seemed to shrink a little in the woman's shadow.

Crash let a small smile cross her lips. She liked Wilder. Wilder didn't talk like an administrator; she sounded like someone well-versed with teenagers and bad attitudes. Knowing that polite language and empathy didn't always work, that sometimes you needed to be as tough as the kids thought they were.

Cassie blinked and swallowed hard. "I don't know. Honest to God. But she's been pissed off about shit, and it's been stewing about for a while."

"Pissed off about what?" Crash said.

"She wouldn't say. Started about a week ago. It was on a Monday, and she showed up with a shitty attitude. I tried to get her to talk about it, but she wouldn't."

"What about other friends? Is there anyone else she would have confided in?"

"No way. Micki, she's locked down that way. She doesn't talk about anything."

"What about a boyfriend? Is she dating someone?"

Cassie cast her eyes sideways, trying to not look at anyone.

"Talk." Wilder's tone meant no nonsense.

Cassie sighed. "There's a guy, okay? But he's one of those guys they tell girls not to date, but that's who we want anyway."

"Who's the boy?"

The girl's shoulders slumped, and she looked down. Crash let her gaze fall to Cassie's sandals. Her toenails were painted black, the polish chipped and worn.

"Billy McCoy," Cassie said.

Wilder looked at Crash. "The McCoy family?"

"Most likely."

Wilder took Cassie by the shoulders. "Thank you, honey. You did the right thing here."

Cassie shirked away. "Yeah, whatever."

Chapter 11

Few companies dealt with private security systems in Parker County; Matt imagined the demand wasn't high since there wasn't all that many people with enough shit to worry about anything getting stolen. Technology had developed anyway. It was easy to buy cameras online, hook them up to a computer, and record things that way. Which Matt thought was a great idea until someone broke in and stole the computer connected to the cameras. Someone Campbell's generation, though, he'd go old-school, pay for professionals.

Matt made the calls from his office and told whoever answered that he was the sheriff investigating a break-in, and he wanted to know if Gary Campbell was a client of theirs so he could see the footage from the video cameras. Call after call, he got nothing.

Then he hit pay dirt.

"Tri-Comm Security Services. This is Joyce speaking. How may I help you?" The woman sounded young and perky, and it wore on an already-exhausted Matt. The day had been a long one between visiting Campbell, stopping by the courthouse to sign off on some paperwork, and then going back to the office. It didn't take much to tire him out these days.

Matt gave his spiel, and the woman said she'd connect him with a support specialist. The person who answered said his name was Doug Jones, and he had a tone of overdone enthusiasm, like the guy at church who leads the deacons or organizes

Boy Scout events.

"I'm looking at a home invasion case at a home here in Parker County, and I noticed a security camera setup at the home, but I'm not sure if the system was yours or not. Don't people usually have signs up? 'This house monitored by So-and-So Security'?"

"Some do because they think it'll scare off people. It's why you see people putting up the signs but not getting the systems, though. Other people, they think the signs invite problems. Who's the person in question?"

"Gary Campbell." Matt gave him the address.

Jones tapped on computer keys. "Mr. Campbell is a client. He's got our Silver Star setup. You said this was a home invasion?"

"Yes. He said he and his wife were attacked in their home three nights ago. Busted in through the back door."

Jones made a humming sound. "According to our records here, everything functioned fine that night. Says here that the code for the back door was deactivated and then reactivated. No issues there. And there's camera footage from all three cameras surrounding the house."

"About that footage," Matt said. "Any chance I can have a peek?"

"There is, but it's the homeowner's decision, not mine. It's his system, so I need his authorization to release the footage."

"That's the problem. Mr. Campbell is being…intransigent."

"As may be the case, Sheriff, but I still can't give that to you without Mr. Campbell's approval. You get a court order and I can hand it over, but otherwise, I can't help you."

Matt made a clicking noise with his tongue. "I'll see what I can do."

Matt called the county attorney's office. Foster Nolan, the county prosecutor, was out of the office—at least that's what his assistant said—so Matt left a message for him to call back when he got back. Matt had rested the receiver in its cradle when Crash walked in and said, "Matt, there could be a problem."

Matt leaned back in his chair. "You need to figure out a way to better preface things, Crash. You have this tendency toward walking in and dropping bombs on me, and I'm a man of not great health, so a little warning would be nice if things are turning to shit."

"Micki Miller was dating one of the McCoy boys."

"But then again, sometimes I suppose there's no good way to start it off, so you just shove the whole thing in there."

"Aside from that being the worst way of describing it imaginable, that was my thought too."

If the Millers were known for a willingness to do whatever it took to make a dollar, using something of a shotgun-blast approach to the enterprise, the McCoys' reputation was about focus. They had grown marijuana for decades, and the stories about the family grew as fast as the crop. The patriarch was an old bird named Tennis McCoy, who ran the family business with an iron-handed authority. No one had heard much out of Tennis in months, though. There were rumors—whispers made their way to Matt, and he could have gone straight to the source to get the rumors confirmed but opted to leave that dog alone. Besides, he doubted there were many tears shed over the old man.

"Did you find out anything about the McCoy kid?" Matt said. He and Crash had gone down the street to O'Dell's for lunch. Most of the courthouse workers filtered down that way around the same time, and Matt and Crash were at a table watching the waitresses hustle around, refilling soda glasses and setting down plates of cheeseburgers and salads and cheese fries.

Crash sipped her Diet Coke. "Micki's friend didn't know much about him. He's a few years older. She wasn't sure how they met. She wasn't even sure what he looked like. Just that he and Micki started seeing one another a few weeks back, and Micki is over the moon about him."

"Did she say 'over the moon'?"

"She did not, no."

"I didn't suspect she did. I doubt any teenager has used that term in years. I'm not sure why you even used it."

"Audrey Hepburn said it once. I think."

"You watch Audrey Hepburn movies?"

"I do. I'm a woman with a college degree. When you start off in higher education, they give you that poster from *Breakfast at Tiffany's*, an obsession with pumpkin spice, and an interest in 35-millimeter photography."

"Find much about McCoy?"

"No criminal record. No college. No social media, but neither does Micki."

"The McCoys aren't the tweeting kind."

The waitress brought out their food—cheeseburgers and fries for both. Crash attacked her bacon-and-blue-cheese burger with vigor.

Crash froze in mid-bite when she realized Matt hadn't touched his food and was instead looking at her.

"Something wrong?" she said.

Matt shook his head. "Nope. Continue."

Crash took a bite of the burger, chewed, and swallowed. "You think we should go out to the McCoy place and talk to them?"

"I do not."

"How come?"

"Because I don't want to die any faster than I am already, and going out there is doing nothing but asking to expedite the process."

"But they might know something."

"They may, but if they do, they won't tell us. The McCoys keep the lights on by growing pot. We show up in a cruiser and start asking questions, what do you think their response is going to be?"

"When framed that way, I feel like the response won't be good."

"I doubt they'd shoot us on sight, but they sure as hell won't throw out a welcome mat. Trying to get information out of them that they don't want to give won't do anything but create more problems than we already have."

"Then what do you recommend?"

Matt ate some of his own burger. His had grilled onions on it and a cool pink center. Perfect.

"That after I finish this burger, I call the county attorney's office again and chew Nolan's ass until he gets me a court order for that video from Campbell's house."

"That's not what I'm talking about, Matt."

"I know what you're talking about, and I'm saying we handle the situation we can handle until we figure out what to do about the other situation."

Crash's expression betrayed frustration. Matt drank his Sprite.

"You think there's a proper way of doing this, Crash, and you're not wrong," Matt said. "But it's not the way to go with this circumstance."

"Why not?"

"For the same reason the best way to stop a car isn't driving into a brick wall."

"That makes not one lick of sense, Matt."

Matt glanced at his plate. He wasn't as hungry as he thought—or at least as he felt he should be. The burger was good, but his stomach raged against everything in protest, and he pushed the plate away.

"You remember how we handled the thing with the white supremacists?" he said.

"I held a gun on one of them in the Riverside, so yes, Matt, I remember. I also remember you guys hot-dogged the whole situation, and it pissed off Jackie Hall."

Matt chuckled. "That last part was a bonus. But the thing is, there was no 'by the book' for a situation like that. They'll tell you at the police academy there is, but something like that is its own unique beast, and you treat it that way. The reason it's called 'by the book' is because it's what people expect you to do. Sometimes, you've got to go with the unexpected."

Matt expelled a small burp. Bile. Lunch rolled angrily inside him.

"Or it may not, and those little girls would have died, and the other hostages would have died—" he said.

"Rachel was a hostage. She would have died."

Matt set the flat of his palm down hard on the table. "What we did was take the road less traveled, and that seemed to make the difference."

"You want to work harder to make this car-into-a-brick-wall analogy stick?"

Matt sighed. "Try this: Conventional wisdom says to stop your car, you apply the brakes until the car stops moving. That's one way of doing it. There's also a more extreme way of handling the situation, which is you can drive your car into a brick wall, and that'll do in a pinch if your brakes don't work."

"Talking to the McCoys, that's driving into the brick wall, even though that's what the rules say we're supposed to do."

"Yes."

"So what you're saying is that the rules of normalcy don't apply to the McCoys."

"They do not. There's another way to stop the car, and what we do is find what that way is."

"I don't like this idea that different rules apply to different people, Matt. My thing was always that the law is applied without regard to anything else. Rich or poor, white or black. Lady Justice and the blindfold and all that."

"And that's how it should be, but it's not how it always is." Matt motioned for the waitress to bring the check. "We'll figure it out."

Matt paid for lunch; Crash offered, and Matt laughed it off. On the way out, they spoke to people they recognized from the courthouse and were headed up the street when nausea hit Matt. He rushed into the alley and bent over behind a dumpster and puked.

Crash stood at the alleyway entrance and said nothing. She had seen this before, and she knew Matt well enough to leave him alone. She heard him heaving and retching and the splattering against the pavement.

The vomiting took a while, and when he came back, Matt was as pale as fresh snow, with yellow tendrils of bile and saliva hanging from his lips. He wiped at his face with a handkerchief and blew his nose. His red-rimmed eyes watered. He struggled to smile, to make the situation less uncomfortable, and they walked back to the office without another word.

When he got home that night, he didn't tell Rachel about vomiting, or the call he made to Dr. Fordham once he got back to the office.

All Fordham said was, "Chemo."

"No," Matt said. "I'm holding out on the liver."

"I'm done screwing around, Matt. I'm serious. We need to schedule a start date."

"But I'll lose my hair, and get puffy, and I won't be pretty anymore, Doc."

"But you'll also be less dead. How's dead look on you?"

"Not in my color wheel."

"Then you see my point."

"You are making one, yes."

"Jesus, Mary, and Joe Strummer, this might be a breakthrough."

Matt sighed. "She wants a baby, Doc."

"A lot of women do."

"Me on chemo won't help that happen."

"Not in the short-term, no, but—"

"She's in her forties, and I'm closer to being fifty than not, plus, you know, fucking cancer, so our short-term isn't like most people's."

"Then you need to determine which she wants more: a theoretical baby or an actual living, breathing husband. Also, I'd recommend you smoke pot."

"What the hell kind of doctor are you?"

"The kind who knows it helps with nausea and lack of appetite."

"You don't understand how long I've been a cop, Doc. The whole idea of it pushes against everything I've done for decades now."

"Don't smoke when you're at work and it'll be fine. I would wager you know the places to procure such a thing."

"Through my line of work, you sometimes run across the occasional purveyor of the good tree."

"That sounds fucking embarrassing when you say it. Find yourself a pot dealer. If you use it in the evenings, it will help with the nausea, and you'll be hungry. Have Rachel buy Doritos."

"Should I listen to the Grateful Dead while I smoke it?"

"No one should do that, Matt. The cancer is suffering enough."

At home that night, Rachel talked about her day and made supper and they lay on the couch together, arms wrapped around one another. Rachel curled into him, a movie playing on the TV that neither of them paid attention to.

Sometimes, in moments like this, Matt forgot he had cancer. He forgot about work, about paperwork, and about things he needed to fix in the house and whether they should get a dog—Rachel was rooting for one, in addition to the baby, which Matt chalked up to overcompensation. He forgot about the lingering guilt and worry he had about Carl and what he planned to do with the rest of his life and whether that time was six months or thirty years.

Matt forgot about everything except how wonderful Rachel felt next to him. He wanted to push the pause button and savor the moment as long as he could, no matter how unrealistic the idea was. He knew at best, it was all nothing more than a succession of moments—good and bad—and all he could hope to do was to remember them, to have something to hold on to when the moments that followed weren't as good.

They went to bed and they made out like teenagers, which was sometimes the best Matt could do. He didn't always have the stamina to take it to the next level, and Rachel never pushed, never rushed. She was soft and gentle to him. He didn't let himself get frustrated when things didn't respond the way he thought they should. There had been plenty of times where his cock had just lain there, flaccid, flopped to the side.

This had been part of a learning experience for them both. Rachel had taken it personally at first, that Matt was already losing interest. A talk to Fordham taught them that this was typical with cancer patients. A response brought about by exhaustion.

They developed other techniques. Matt had found other ways to be giving to her, and Rachel, she didn't complain about that. Sometimes they spent half the night kissing and touching one another, a playful exploration that reminded them of what it had been like when they were younger and learning one another's bodies. But this came without the fevered rush of youth, with a gentleness and a sense of contemplation. Matt rediscovered birthmarks on Rachel that he had forgotten about. Rachel found new places on Matt that, with the slightest bit of pressure, elicited gales of ticklish laughter, and sometimes a startling state of arousal.

On those nights, as they slept, they clung to one another as if the other might float away into the night.

Matt's cell phone ringing broke them both of their sleep.

1:18 a.m.

Matt answered. Crash on the other end.

"Everything okay?" Matt said.

"There's been another one," she said.

Chapter 12

The lights were visible long before Matt made the turn up the road toward the house. A mixture of flashing blue lights from police cars and the red lights from EMS. People stood in their front yards, dressed in pajamas and bathrobes, watching it all with that uniquely human combination of compassion and morbid curiosity. Hoping the neighbors were okay and grateful it hadn't been them.

The ambulance pulled out of the driveway, the siren screaming to life as it passed Matt, leaving him a space to park his cruiser. Several of the cruisers already there belonged to the state police, and a knot wrestled in his stomach.

Crash stood at the head of the driveway, talking to another deputy and a pair of uniformed state troopers. Matt's cruiser slid into the space, and Crash rushed to catch him as he exited the car.

"He's here." Her voice was hushed, almost whispered. "Jackie Hall."

Matt slammed the car door harder than he intended. "What happened?"

"Same M.O. as before. Attackers were waiting for the victims in the house as they were coming home." She motioned to the road. "That ambulance you passed was taking them to the hospital." A beat. "They were coming back from visiting grandchildren."

"How bad this time?"

"They pistol-whipped them both. The husband got the brunt of it this time. The wife, she's younger—looks like she was a trophy at one time—and she took it better than he did." Crash looked back to the house. "Couple's name is Peter and Kara Carlton. He's late sixties, and she's maybe fifty, I'm guessing. They had a dog. A golden retriever. The wife said the dog always barked when they came home, but they got inside, and he wasn't there. That's when they realized something was wrong." Crash's voice sharpened. "We found the dog in the backyard. It looks like they beat it to death with a baseball bat."

"Jesus."

"Yeah, I'll say they may have called on him, but he didn't answer the phone."

"Let's keep the blasphemy minimal tonight, Crash. We need everyone we can get rooting for our side." Matt's eyes shifted over to the state troopers. They were young—neither of them looked more than twenty-five—and they were built like bouncers at a bar, with shoulders broad and straight. It was as if they had broom handles strapped back there. Their uniforms were crisp and fit well, and they wore their flat-brimmed hats low over their eyes.

Crash turned to her notebook. "State police was here when I got here."

"They been behaving themselves?"

"They're good kids. They're young."

Matt laughed. "Have you suddenly progressed to being a wise sage?"

"Not really, but I'd bet I'm more badass than either of them."

"A breeze could knock you over, Crash."

"I'm small, but I'm mighty." She bared her teeth like a dog readying for a fight and growled.

"I'm terrified." Matt twisted his head around. "Where's Hall at?"

"Inside. He was talking to the wife." Crash flipped pages on her notebook. "He seems like a nice guy, Matt."

Matt ignored the comment. "How's the wife seem?"

"As fine as you can be after watching your husband get beaten."

"She know about the dog?"

"It seemed like a lot to dump on her all at once."

"She back up what Campbell told us?"

Crash shook her head. "She said there were only two of them. And they asked about money from 'the Guthrie job.'"

Matt wrote the phrase down in his notebook and underlined it for emphasis. "What the hell does that mean?"

"Well, shit, Matt, if I knew, it might suck the mystery out of all this."

"Did Carlton or his wife have a clue what they were talking about?"

"Mrs. Carlton was in hysterics. They tried talking to her, but she was on the floor next to her husband, sobbing." Crash swallowed hard. "They smeared shit on the walls like before, but the violence on the victims escalated. There's blood on the walls. The wife, she'll be in the hospital for a while, but the husband, he's not leaving."

Matt heaved a deep breath. "Only two attackers? You think someone broke away from the group? Or are these two going off on their own?"

"I don't know. I'll be honest, Matt, that this is outside of anything I imagined going on here. This is what you hear about happening in other places, the stories parents tell their kids so they don't move off to the big, bad city."

"Those are thin lines these days. The shit we always thought made us better than those places, that's hanging outside our back doors."

A large shadow fell through the open front door, and behind it came Lieutenant Jackie Hall. Hall was a big man dressed in a white short-sleeved dress shirt, the underarms stained yellow, and a flowered blue tie and shiny gray slacks. He wore his shield on a lanyard, the badge resting on top of his ample gut. He ran his ham-sized hand over the top of his close-cropped blond hair and saw Matt, giving him a big smile like they were the best friends on earth.

Hall made his way over, and the closer he got, the more Matt could see how red and flushed the big man's face was. He huffed a few breaths of air and placed his hand on the hood of Matt's cruiser, shifting his weight over to that side, and Matt heard the car's suspension whine like a whipped puppy.

"How you doing, Sheriff?" Hall said.

The contents of Matt's stomach soured.

"I'm great, Lieutenant. How are you?"

"Couldn't be better. Just waiting on the baby to show up."

"Didn't know you were expecting. How far along are you?"

Hall laughed and winked and pointed a finger at Matt. "Forgot what a funny guy you are."

"Just laughing to hide the tears."

"My missus, she's due here soon. A little girl. We got our boy already, so this'll give us the bookends."

"That's wonderful, Lieutenant. Good for you. So, about this attack. I understand you spoke to Mrs. Carlton."

"Wouldn't call much of that 'talking.' She wasn't in a state to say much. I suppose I'll go over to the hospital and see if I can get a statement. Your chief deputy here—" He jerked his head toward Crash. "She said you had a situation similar a few nights ago. Kind of shocked you didn't send a report over our way. We'd be more than happy to hop in on this with you."

"Didn't seem like much. Home invasion. We figured it was kids doing stupid shit. Probably drugs involved. We've been working the case."

"From the looks of inside the house, I'd guess drugs played a role here also. You don't create that kind of chaos without being in an altered state." Hall lifted himself up from the car hood, and the car groaned in appreciation. "You think you could send over the preliminary you've got on the previous case?"

Matt raised an eyebrow. "Is the state police interested in taking over this case?"

"Not if your boys have a handle on it. I'd like to check over what work you've got and see if there's anything we can contribute. If this was the second attack, you've got to think there'll be a third."

"I'll have Crash e-mail it to you first thing in the morning."

The smile that broke across Hall's face pushed back at folds of fat and flesh, and it made him look like a jovial egg. "Why do they call you 'Crash,' Deputy?"

Crash didn't look amused. Her face was as hard and blank as a brick wall. "People just have weird senses of humor, that's all."

"I guess they do." Hall nodded in agreement. "I guess they do." He peered back at the house. "I'll check back in there with the deputies. You kids have a good night."

"You too, Lieutenant," Matt said.

"I've told you before, call me Jackie. Everyone else does."

"Sure thing, Lieutenant." Matt smiled. "I mean, Jackie."

Hall turned and walked away, disappearing back into the house.

Matt stared at the front of the house for a beat. Crash watched him, waiting.

"You know what I hate to think about, Crash?" he said.

"I cringe at the possibilities."

"That there's a good chance he'll outlive me. It might only be by ten or fifteen minutes, but it's likely to happen."

"Are the state boys going to snag this from us?"

"Don't know. I'd prefer they didn't."

"You really don't like him, do you?"

"Not even a little bit."

"Any particular reason?"

"Do I need one?"

"Common decorum and logic would say you rationally need

a reason to dislike someone. But I'm not one to tell you how to live your life, either, Matt."

"Thank you."

"We need to find out what the Guthrie job is."

"We do."

"That means talking to Campbell again."

"I show up at that man's door much more, I'll have to bring a covered dish."

Crash covered her notebook and leaned against Matt's cruiser. "I don't like this, Matt. Something bad is going on here."

Matt looked at the flashing lights moving across the side of the house then looked at the neighbors watching it all—they probably wondered if they would feel safe when they went back inside and turned the final locks before trying to go back to sleep for the night.

Chapter 13

Matt came into the office the next morning and found out Foster Nolan had already called and left him a voice mail with a request to call him. It was just past eight.

Matt set his to-go cup of Sheetz coffee on his desk and called Nolan. Nolan's assistant connected him.

"Jesus, Sheriff, why didn't you tell me what the hell was going on here?" Nolan's voice was panicked as though he were trying to convince the bank not to foreclose on the family farm.

"Good morning to you too, Foster. And to what do I owe this pleasure?"

"When you called about that court order for the video, I didn't realize what the fuck was happening."

"Foster, I appreciate your sudden concern about my investigation, but can you cool your jets long enough to tell me what's got you wound this tight?"

There was a sigh on the other end of the line. "I read about the break-in that happened overnight. I'm putting in with Judge Bailey for the court order to get the video footage you requested."

"There's something about the attack last night already?"

"On the *Herald-Tribune* website. Everyone in the office was talking about it when I came in this morning. Haven't you read it yet?"

"My coffee's not even at a drinkable temperature yet, Foster. I don't read anything until then."

"You need to check it out. I told Bailey to have the order ready for one of your deputies by eleven so you can deliver it to the company before lunch."

"That's a hell of a lot of hustle."

"Old people attacked in their own homes—that'll scare people. Matt, fear is a good motivator for many things."

Matt couldn't argue that point.

Matt drove to Parker County General around lunchtime while Crash headed out to get the court order and go by Tri-Comm. Tri-Comm's main office was the next county over, in Lyons.

Like everyone, he supposed, Matt had no great love for hospitals. When he first got sick, when he had body aches and fevers and was dropping weight, he came to Parker General, to the walk-in clinic, and everyone had thought he had the flu. Then he turned shades of yellow, and Rachel made him see "a real doctor," she said. He had always been healthy, had always taken care of himself—ever since his army days.

Matt had been military police. Other guys he worked with gained weight—told themselves that bulk was the same thing as muscle—and Matt knew that was a mistake since the job meant dealing with combat-trained soldiers who knew those Jack Reacher methods of how to take out six guys in a fight single-handed. Matt had seen that shit go down, and he did not want to be the guy sucking back his pride and spitting out loose teeth at the end of the fight.

So he ran and hit the gym, and he never reached the point of being a muscle head, but he kept solid and could handle himself in a brawl. When he left the military and he and Rachel came back to Parker County and he got elected sheriff, he still put in the time; part of what had put him in office was that people liked this guy who took care of himself, who hadn't gone to seed like a lot of ex-military. There was vanity, sure; he wouldn't deny that since he liked how he filled out the uniform. Well past forty, and he wasn't anything to be ashamed of.

That had been before the cancer. Losing weight. Wondering how much longer he had. Walking into the hospital today, he caught his reflection in the glass, and he didn't know who the hell this person was that he was looking at. Every time this happened, it caught him off guard, and he worked not to let it affect him. Some days were better than others, and today in the sheriff's department polo shirt and black slacks, was one of the others.

A young nurse at the front desk told Matt that Peter Carlton was in the ICU, and she gave him directions, which he didn't need. He'd been there so many times before, coming to interview someone after an accident, after an assault, but he took the directions with a smile and an appreciative nod.

He paused at the door to Carlton's room when he heard voices. He recognized Jackie Hall as one of them; the other was a woman's, soft, almost a whisper. He guessed Kara Carlton. Anger coiled inside him, and he exhaled deeply, trying to let go of that sense of Hall treading in on his case.

Matt pushed the door open and walked in. Kara Carlton sat in a chair and Jackie Hall stood over her, almost looming, his back to Matt. Hall wore a gray suit, and Matt could see the seams running up the back of the jacket, ready to pop at a moment's notice.

A litany of machines spread out from Peter Carlton like a medical spiderweb. He looked older than Matt had expected but like one of those guys aging into Ernest Hemingway, with a head of snow-white hair and a bushy beard the same color. Someone who spent weekends fishing or camping, maybe woodworking or rebuilding an old pickup, Matt thought. The guy Matt had expected himself to age into.

Carlton's eyes were shut, and a ventilator hissed as it breathed for him, its sound intertwined with the beep of a heart monitor. Several IVs ran into his arm, their dripping drumming a steady beat.

"Would you recognize their voices again, Mrs. Carlton?" Hall said.

"I believe so. It...it was a lot, Lieutenant." She choked on her words. "All I remember is them hitting Peter. They kept hitting him over and over, asking the same thing over and over."

Matt stepped farther into the room and cleared his throat. Jackie Hall twisted around and gave a nod and a head jerk to Matt to come in. The movements caused the rolls of fat on the back of his head to clump together and fold over the collar of his shirt.

Kara Carlton craned her head around Jackie Hall to see Matt. Not knowing the situation, Matt would have guessed her to be the daughter, not the wife. She was on the far end of forty, close to where Matt was parked, a redhead dressed in an ice cream-colored linen dress. She wore minimal makeup except for dark eyeliner and cherry red lipstick, and it accentuated the paleness of her face. Some of that eyeliner had streaked and raced down her face now, and she attempted to blot it away with a tissue.

Matt reached a hand out to her. "Mrs. Carlton, I'm Sheriff Matt Simms. My department's involved in the investigation into the attack last night."

Kara Carlton shook his hand. "Thank you, Sheriff. Lieutenant Hall said another family was attacked a few nights ago."

Matt nodded. "We believe it to be the same perpetrators."

"Do you have any idea who's doing this?"

"We're developing leads and some suspects. You said there were two attackers last night?"

Jackie Hall said, "Mrs. Carlton and I, we've already gone over all of this. Rather than continuing to upset her, I can just pass on my notes to you—"

"If you don't mind, Lieutenant, I'd like to hear from Mrs. Carlton personally about what happened." Matt's tone was firm, no-nonsense. He was in no mood to deal with Jackie Hall, and his words edged that out more than he liked. He looked at

Kara Carlton and turned on a smile intended to feel empathetic and understanding. "If Mrs. Carlton is comfortable talking about it."

She pulled another tissue from a box and dabbed away at her face. "If it will help, Sheriff." She blew her nose into the tissue. It was a delicate, overly feminine sound. "We came home from dinner. Peter likes this steakhouse in Morgantown, and we go there and see his son and the son's wife and their children. We came in through the front door, and Molly—that's our golden lab—she didn't show up when we walked in. Peter thought she might just be sleeping, but it didn't feel right. Molly is as dumb as a stump, but she's loyal, and she's always at the door when we come home.

"We walked into the living room, and there was someone sitting there on the couch, smoking a cigarette like they lived there. He had his ski mask on over half of his face but hooked up above his nose so he could smoke. And Peter and I stared at the guy. He sat there like he owned the place, like this was normal.

"Peter's got a permit for a concealed carry, and he wears it with him whenever we go out. He had it clipped to his belt, and he reached for it but before he got to it, he screamed and fell over. I saw something in the corner of my eye. Someone with a baseball bat had been in a corner of the room and I never saw him. They pointed the end at me and said—" Her face tightened. "They said, 'Sit the fuck down, bitch.'"

"Do you remember what they wore?" Matt said.

"The guy on the couch, he had on blue jeans and a black T-shirt. And the ski mask. The guy who hit Peter, he wore a sweatshirt and blue jeans."

"What kind of sweatshirt? WVU or Marshall? A high school?"

"Just a gray sweatshirt, Sheriff. Plain gray. The person with the baseball bat, they told me to sit down. His voice, it sounded funny. He was trying to make it sound deep, like he wanted to disguise it. The one who was smoking, he stood up and pushed me down onto the couch. He did the rest of the talking."

"The person with the baseball bat say anything else?"

"Not a word." She swallowed hard and wiped a tear from her cheek. "He kept hitting Peter with the bat. The other person, he kept asking about 'the Guthrie job.' He would ask Peter about the money from the Guthrie job."

"What did your husband tell them?"

"Nothing. He said he didn't know what they were talking about, and then they'd hit him again." She let out a soft sob she tried to choke back without success. "I saw the red of the bat when they swung at Peter again, and I realized what happened to Molly." She swallowed again. "Then the red, it got worse, and that was coming from Peter."

Matt crouched down low to meet Kara at eye level. "What does your husband do for a living?"

"He owned a trucking company. He was the vice president and ran the books for years, but he sold out his share and retired when he met me." Her eyes went to the hospital bed, and her face softened, and a smile crept across her lips. "He told me he'd spent all of those early years working to build his business, and he'd missed out on a lot of life then with his first wife, with his kids. He told me he didn't want to repeat those mistakes with me."

Matt nodded. He took Kara s'hand and gave it a gentle squeeze. "We will catch the people who did this, Mrs. Carlton."

Her smile turned wan and half-hearted. "Thank you, Sheriff."

Jackie Hall followed Matt out of the hospital room. He said, "Jesus but this, it's something, ain't it?"

Matt sighed a sound of weariness. He felt tired on a bone-deep level—beyond cancer and nights of shitty, half-hearted sleep and the general exhaustion of dealing with life and the world and the bullshit that people insisted on pumping into it.

"Everything is always something, Lieutenant," he said. "That's what makes things *things*."

"That's almost philosophical sounding."

"I've got my moments, I suppose."

They walked down the hall until they got to the coffee machine. It was an ancient model that dispensed coffee or what was claimed to be a "cappuccino." The machine was so old that the photo displays had long turned yellow. Jackie Hall fished around in his pants—one eye closed, tongue clenched between his teeth—and brought out a handful of change. He pumped coins into the machine and ordered up a cup with extra sweetener, extra creamer. The cup dropped into the dispenser and filled with a muddy brown solution that Matt supposed was, on some molecular level, coffee.

Jackie Hall gave the cup a sniff. Matt could smell it too, and he tried to hide his disgust as Hall sipped the coffee and made a satisfied sigh.

"I had someone tell me to never get coffee out of these machines," Matt said. "It's nothing but syrups that get blended together, so it's not really coffee. Plus, they don't get cleaned often, so you end up with a sludge milkshake that's also the detritus of maybe ten years' worth of other people's alleged cups of coffee."

Jackie Hall listened to Matt, looked at the cup's contents, shrugged, and took another drink. "Do I look like a man awash with health concerns, Sheriff?"

"I guess not."

"I am not, though my wife, she's got plenty for me, and she's forever telling me what I'm doing wrong and what I'm doing right, and let me assure you the wrong always outweighs the right." Jackie drank more coffee. "I'm hoping here you might have some insight into what they're talking about with the Guthrie job."

"Sounds criminal. Sounds like what someone in a TV show would call something criminal."

"That's my thoughts. That's how they're always referring to things in movies, on TV. It's always a *job*, like it's real work. If it was real work, they'd be paying taxes."

"There it's a big heist, something perfectly planned and executed, and they're the good guys and we're the bad guys, and you're supposed to be rooting for them to get away with the money."

"While in real life, it's usually some idiot with a sawed-off shotgun going into a convenience store and stealing fifty bucks out of the register and a bag of pork rinds."

At the elevator, Matt pushed the call button and waited for the doors to open. Inside the elevator car, not even meaning to, Matt glanced at the weight limit. Even with just the two of them in there, the elevator car seemed tight and confined. Jackie Hall consumed space without effort or concern.

There was silence as the elevator rode to the first floor and came to a stop, wobbling a little before the doors opened. The two men looked at one another.

"Are you guys taking over the investigation?" Matt said as they stepped out of the elevator.

Jackie shook his head. "Your department caught it and seems to have a handle on it. I'd not mind working with you, sharing resources and whatnot."

Matt told Jackie about the video footage Crash was picking up from Tri-Comm.

Jackie said, "Let me know what comes out of that. Mrs. Carlton said they didn't have any security setup, so whatever your video shows might be all we have so far. Anything we can do to help, you let us know. I think we can trade the information back and forth, and if someone thinks of something, just pass it along. You have a good one, Sheriff."

"You too, Lieutenant."

"Someday, I'll get you to call me Jackie. It's what all my friends do." Jackie Hall laughed and walked away, and Matt watched at the man's large shadow disappear out the hospital doors and fade out into nothing.

Chapter 14

Tri-Comm's offices were in a two-story brick building that also housed several sets of doctors and lawyers offices. Crash wore her hat in, the paperwork in a manila envelope underneath her arm. The front of Tri-Comm looked like every waiting room she had ever spent time in, with motel room chairs and out-of-date magazines on the end tables. A soft rock station out of Clarksburg was playing overhead, and Crash recognized the Celine Dion song from *Titanic*. She grimaced at the recognition; she hated that fucking song.

The woman at the desk was in her mid-fifties, officious looking, in a tweed-looking suit and a blouse with a big puff at the chest, her unnaturally black hair short and hairsprayed hard into place. She glanced up from her phone call, noticed Crash, and gave a nod, then said into the phone, "Georgia, I've got to go. Tell me what you decide on for the dinner and give me a ring this evening. Okay? Okay? No, that's fine, Georgia. Really. Really, I've got to go. Ball's in your court. You'll do fine, I promise. I've got to go, Georgia. Seriously, you decide and you let me know. Okay. Talk to you then. Bye." She placed the phone back into its cradle and rolled her eyes. "Some people." She flashed a smile and said, "Can I help you, Deputy?"

Crash said, "I hope so," and reached the manila envelope out to her. "That's a court order for system footage we need for an investigation. I'm delivering it to Mr. Jones."

THE RIGHTEOUS PATH

The papers were all from Judge Ottermein's office, on a light gray paper that was a heavier stock, stamped and looking official. The woman put on a pair of glasses, flipped through the papers, replaced everything into the envelope, and said, "I'll be right back," and disappeared into another office.

Crash bobbed back and forth on the balls of her feet while the radio station went from Celine Dion to some boy band she hated to admit she knew. It was a newer song, though it could have been something she had listened to a decade prior, before she had discovered black fingernail polish and Nine Inch Nails. She wondered why boy bands always seemed to sound the same, regardless of when they came out. The music got a little slicker, the production heavier, but at its core, it was always the same song about loving a girl or losing a girl or spending a lifetime with a girl, all songs focused and designed to make girls feel special and unique—just the same way another girl had felt years before.

The woman walked out of the office, followed by a man. Forties, graying, mustache, the look of a studious follower of rules. Dressed in a short-sleeve shirt and tie and dark slacks with white specks, Crash identified the signs of cat ownership.

The woman sat back down behind the desk, whereas the man came around and shook Crash's hand and identified himself as Doug Jones. "How you doing today, Deputy?"

"Outstanding. Yourself?"

"Outside of the police showing up at work, I'm great." He said it with a slight chuckle, like he knew it wasn't funny but hoped she would laugh anyway. She didn't. He pulled the court order from the envelope. His eyes darted across the paperwork. "If you don't mind, I need to have our attorney look this over."

"It's a black-and-white issue, Mr. Jones. We need that security footage of the Campbell house from the night of the attack."

He smiled. "I understand that, honey, but—"

"Try again," Crash said.

Jones looked confused. "Excuse me?"

"Please finish what you were saying."

Jones ruffled the papers. "What I'm saying, sweetheart, is—"

Crash smiled that smile that wasn't meant to be funny. "That right there. You can address me as 'Deputy' or 'Chief Deputy Landing.' Call me 'honey' or 'sweetheart' one more time, and we'll have problems."

Jones's eyes swelled with surprise. "I meant nothing by that…Deputy." He cleared his throat. "I need to make sure we're in the clear with this. Our attorney, he's out of town right now. I can have this scanned and e-mailed to him. Once he calls me back, I'll hand you over the footage."

She handed him a business card. "My cell number is on there. You call me as soon as your attorney gives you the okay on this. Understand that people's lives are at risk here. There's been two attacks. If there's a third, and you could have helped prevent it, I'll make sure you're charged with obstruction of justice. And I'll put cuffs on you myself."

"Is it the policy of the sheriff's department to threaten people?"

"Of the department, no. Not my policy either. But I'll make sure it's a promise I keep." Crash leaned around and looked at the woman at the desk. She had watched everything with the slightest of grins on her face. Crash tipped her hat toward her. "You have a good day, ma'am," she said and walked out the door.

Chapter 15

Parker County High School let out at 2:45 p.m. Crash got there a few minutes before the final bell rang, parked across the street in the parking lot of a pizza place, and leaned against the cruiser so she could watch students file out of the building. It was a torrent of faces. Almost all white, because Parker County was one of the most homogenous counties in the United States—Crash was sure she had read that online, though she supposed that, since the election, you needed to question almost anything you read online.

Some kids filtered onto the school buses lined up in front of the building. Other kids—better dressed, carrying themselves with a confidence that spoke of privilege—they headed into the student parking lot and got into pickup trucks and newer-model cars. A few kids walked over and into the pizza place. They paused at the sight of Crash, her arms folded across her chest, looking defiant and nonchalant. She gave them a quick nod, and they whispered to themselves and went inside, and she returned her focus to across the street.

Crash watched Cassie Peters leave the school. She seemed small and frightened, her head sunk low between her shoulders and her books clutched close to her chest like she wanted to will herself to be invisible. No one talked to her as she stepped out into the sunlight and made her way through the throngs of people, dodging contact with anyone, pushing forward and away from everyone, as if touching them would infect her with something fatal.

In that kid's mind, it just might, Crash thought.

Cassie didn't get on the bus but instead checked traffic both ways with a practiced eye and crossed the street. That was when she saw Crash—as her feet hit the sidewalk. She paused and stared at her.

Crash smiled. Cassie did not.

Crash pushed herself off the hood of the cruiser. "How are you doing, Cassie?"

"Fine." Cassie's face twisted into a scowl. She looked like she'd realized someone next her had just passed gas.

"Good to hear. How was school?"

"Fine."

"That'll be the response for any question I ask, won't it?"

Cassie shrugged. Students from the high school continued to walk over. They slowed down and whispered to one another at the sight of Crash and Cassie talking.

Crash moved toward Cassie. Cassie leaned away from her.

"Can we go somewhere and talk?" Crash said.

"What about?"

"About Micki."

"I already told you the other day I don't know anything."

"I know, but I'm hoping maybe you'll remember something. Kids remember plenty when they don't have other people around." Crash craned her head toward the pizza place. "Hungry? We can get a slice."

Cassie smirked. "Great fucking idea. That'll look great tomorrow morning. There'll be new levels of social martyrdom for me. I'm sure there's a deeper pit they can throw me into."

"What about somewhere else? You like burgers?"

Cassie seemed to give it thought and glanced back over her shoulder. Groups of kids watched the proceedings from the front of the school and through school bus windows.

"I'm already dead," she said. "Why not let them throw more

dirt on me?"

She walked toward the back of the cruiser and had her hand on the handle when Crash said, "You can ride up front."

"No thanks. If they're going to talk about me, I might as well give them a good story." She opened the door and slid into the back.

In the most technical of senses, Tully's was a bar and shouldn't have let Cassie in, but Tully was working behind the counter when Crash and Cassie showed up, and he waved them through. He gave them a nod and a smile as he wiped down the counter with a rag that didn't look clean to begin with. He was a chunky guy on the other side of life, bald with a shaggy rim of yellow-white hair and a face dusted with snowy stubble and aged by decades spent in the darkened confines of the bar.

The place was empty that afternoon except for two guys sipping on beers and watching the Pirates game on the TV. "Hotel California" blasted from the jukebox, drowning out the play-by-play.

"The usual, Crash?" Tully said.

"Two of 'em. And make the fries crispy." To Cassie, she said, "What you want to drink?"

"Cranberry and vodka."

"Funny. Coke? Sprite? Diet?"

"Coke."

Crash held up two fingers. "Two Cokes."

From underneath the counter, Tully brought out an apron he pulled on over a stained Steelers T-shirt. "Sure thing."

They sat as far away from the bar and jukebox noise as possible. Cassie, on the side opposite from Crash, had her eyes downward, her body folded in on itself. Crash placed her hat on the table. Cassie glanced over at it. She lifted her head and moved her gaze to Crash. Her face seemed flush with a distant curiosity, as if there were questions she wanted to ask, but they seemed too theoretical to be important.

"You always this quiet?" Crash said.

"Not always."

"Today you are."

"How many kids you talk to that want to talk to cops?"

"Not very many. People start feeling guilty, they talk to the police."

"I didn't do anything to feel guilty about."

"Never said you did. But police make everyone nervous. We show up when bad shit goes down. It doesn't always make us popular at parties."

Cassie tilted her head to the side and pushed her mouth into a bow.

"Why'd you become a cop?" she said.

"Because I wanted to do the right thing for people and make sure other people did the right thing, and if they didn't, then catch them before they did anything else wrong."

"I bet that answer goes over great when you talk to third graders and all, but I'm serious. You're a woman. There wasn't something else you wanted to do with your life but hang out in this shithole, deal with asshole drunks and other pieces of white trash?"

"You're not on the pep squad, are you?"

Cassie folded her arms across her chest. "I hate this fucking town. Everything about it, and every person here."

"You didn't hate Micki."

"Micki hated it here too. Sometimes all you need in your friends is to hate the same shit as you."

Crash pointed at Cassie's T-shirt. It was the Ramones, the picture of the four of them standing against a brick wall. "Being punk rock around here doesn't make life simpler, either."

"Only thing around here are cowboy hat-wearing assholes, listening to fucking Toby Keith and that ignorant shit, or you've got these stupid-ass white boys blasting Kendrick Lamar and acting thug when they're nothing but crackers in a double-wide in the middle of B.F.E. And the girls are bowheads, talking about Rihanna and Beyonce like they understand anything they're talking about, or they're fucking racists who think we need to send people back to Africa." She shook her head in disgust. "If me wondering why anyone would stay here seems weird, I'm sorry, but you must be broken somewhere inside to choose living here, because most bitches who stay in Parker County are married by the time they're eighteen and pumping out kids, or they're going to church and waiting for a deacon to propose, or they're jacked up on five or six different prescriptions. Unless they're doing heroin, which, Jesus Christ, just fucking die already."

Crash leaned back in her chair. "Goddamn. That must be exhausting."

"What?"

"Sitting around all day putting people into little boxes that way. How do you find the time to do anything else?"

Cassie glared at her with cold, hard eyes. To Crash, it was funny, this girl putting on this show of being such a hard ass. It felt familiar.

She jutted her chin out toward Cassie's T-shirt. "You like them?"

Cassie shook her head, not in a dismissal but to bring herself back to the here and now. She had to look down at the front of her shirt and gave an offhanded shrug. "They're good. I like the old stuff."

"What else do you listen to?"

"Skinny Puppy, the Stooges, the Clash, Sex Pistols."

"Old school. I can appreciate that. You listen to anything new?"

"A little. Like, on Pandora or Spotify."

"It's nice you've got that. In my day, you scouted them out on YouTube. Before that, you had to hope MTV played their video."

"MTV used to play videos?" She said it with a straight face, but then it was as though she couldn't help herself and a smile appeared. It was a nice smile, one that Crash imagined the girl worked hard never to use.

Tully came out with the Cokes. He nudged at Cassie's shoulder with his elbow. "You should watch who you hang out with, young lady." He shot a quick glance over to Crash, then leaned into Cassie. In an exaggerated whisper, he said, "This one, she's trouble. Spends her time around a suspicious crowd."

"You can't whisper for shit, Tully." Crash sipped at her soda. "You should try using syrup in this sometime. Some actual Coke in here would bring out the flavor."

Tully shook his head. "See what I have to deal with? The police acting like they own the world."

"Those burgers done burning yet or what?"

Tully looked at Crash with a stern expression that was an obvious sham. "You kids today have no respect."

Crash's smile was slow and easy, playful, with a twinkle in her eye. This was the game they always played. They knew their parts.

"This joint classes up by half when I show up," she said.

"I'll have you know I run a classy joint. Now if you don't mind, I've gotta go empty the rat traps before I bring you your burgers."

He headed back to the bar.

Cassie said, "He was joking about the rat trap, right?"

"Most likely. I don't think he'd empty it until after he brought the burgers out."

"You're still joking, right?"

"Maybe I am. Maybe I'm not. Who's to say." Crash took another drink of her Coke. "God but that is terrible."

Cassie drank some of hers. The drink was tentative and cautious, as if the beverage might bite back. "That *is* bad."

"I would not lie to you."

There was a beat—a momentary pause where her guard went down and she seemed to consider Crash's words—before Cassie curled her mouth into that smirk again. "You say that, but it's like people asking them to trust you. If you have to ask to be trusted, then you can't be trusted."

"Christ, kid, but how did you get so fucking cynical so young?"

Tully brought them their food before Cassie could answer. That was, if she would answer. Or even if she had an answer.

About the burgers: they were half the size of the plates they rested on, with the fries filling up the remaining space. The fries were hand cut and dark brown, almost burnt. Tully placed a bottle of ketchup on the table between them and waited.

Crash lifted the bun and checked everything out. "I see you're using the fresh lettuce today."

"It's something crazy I thought I'd try."

"Kudos on that."

"Everything looks good?"

"Looks great, Tully."

Crash popped open the lid on the ketchup and squeezed out the bottle's contents until the fries had almost vanished underneath a flood of pureed tomatoes and corn syrup. She fished a few fries out of the mess and ate them. The crunch was audible even over the sound of Three Dog Night playing from the jukebox.

Crash took a large bite of the burger. It was delicious, and she chewed the bite with an ecstasy she did not try to hide. There were plenty of places to get a decent burger in Parker County—Matt's friend Henry had mentioned another beer joint to try—but for Crash's money, Tully's was the best.

She looked over and saw half of Cassie's burger already gone. The girl ate with a furiousness more appropriate for predators in a *National Geographic* documentary. She kept her eyes down, focused on the food, and didn't pause long between bites. Cassie wasn't the first hungry kid she had brought to Tully's for a cheeseburger, and Crash was confident she wouldn't be the last, but she didn't remember the last time one of them had been this hungry. This was how you ate if you thought the food might be taken from you, or there might not be food again.

Crash focused back on her own burger, and no one spoke as they ate until Crash finished hers, and she saw Cassie working through the fries. Crash wiped the grease off her fingers with a napkin and pushed her plate across the table.

"I can't finish 'em, if you want 'em," she said.

Cassie paused with a fry in mid-air. "You sure?"

"Yeah. I don't need 'em anyway."

Cassie finished her fries and the rest of Crash's, then sat there staring at the empty plates. Her face trembled, and her eyes grew wide and glossy with tears. Her voice cracked. "I'm...I'm sorry."

Crash fought the urge to come out of the chair and hold the girl, to put her arms around her and squeeze her tight. *Give her some space*, she thought. *Let her have her moment.*

"For what?" Crash said.

Cassie shuddered. "I'm just...sorry."

That was when it happened. Cassie broke down into tears. She pushed her face into her hands and smothered the sounds. The music—now it was Journey, telling everyone to not stop believin'—did its part, but it wasn't enough, and Cassie trembled in her chair, sucking in air through her nose, making a huge, wet sound.

From the bar, a drinker looked toward them, an acknowledgment of something happening, then turned back to watching the game.

Crash brought her chair around to Cassie and sat close to her. Cassie leaned forward and placed her face on Crash's shoulder and sobbed harder, taking hold of her shoulders as if she needed to keep herself steady. Crash reached around and patted the teenager on the back, between the shoulder blades, and remained otherwise motionless, just letting her cry.

The Frosty Mart wasn't very far from Tully's, so once Cassie had gone to the bathroom and washed her face off and felt like she seemed somewhat presentable, they drove in that direction. They went through the drive-through, Cassie getting a Whirlwind with chunks of Kit Kat blended with vanilla soft serve, and Crash getting a chocolate-dipped cone, then sat in the empty parking lot, eating their ice cream.

"Your parents not wondering where you'ree at?" Crash said.

Cassie stirred her ice cream. "Doubtful they're even home."

"Work?"

Cassie coughed out a noise that could have been a laugh. "Yeah, that's a big fucking joke right there." She took a bite of her ice cream. "Mom, she's not had a job as long as I can remember. Dad, jobs come and go whenever the mines are hiring, and they ain't hiring."

"Where are they then?"

"I'd guess Mom is at church praying for everyone's souls, and afterward she'll get fucked by the preacher because he's that kind of asshole, and Dad's somewhere drinking and losing money he doesn't have at playing cards, too stupid to realize those guys cheat on account they know he's stupid. It's a vicious cycle that way."

Crash nodded and crunched on a bite of the ice cream shell. She kept her tone cool, even, nonjudgmental. "Siblings?"

She shook her head. "That's how Mom ended up going to church all the time, was because she kept having miscarriages. Doctors weren't even sure I'd make it out. Then after me, she couldn't get pregnant again, but instead of going to doctors, Mom found Jesus, and Jesus decided that it wasn't happening again for Donny and Claire Peters."

"You're not a believer?"

"It's all bullshit. Mom told me I had to go. She wanted us to look like those happy little families you see on TV shows. But everyone there's nothing but a hypocrite and a kiss-ass. I watched these snotty brats show up on Sunday morning, acting all high and mighty and pious, no matter what they'd been doing Friday and Saturday night. I couldn't stomach it, so I said I wasn't going anymore. Mom threw a shit fit, told me I'd go to hell if I didn't straighten up my attitude. I told her she should stop bending over and taking it up the ass for Brother Roger."

"That go over well?"

"She slapped me so hard, my ears rang for two days."

"This how you and Micki got to be friends? You both being the rebellious types?"

"I guess. Neither one of us can stand it around here. Everyone's such a fucking phony, and there's this idea you got to be or do this certain type of person to fit in, and fuck it all if you're not willing to do those things."

"You mean like the rich kids?"

Cassie shrugged. "I suppose so. You ever wonder why you look around and it seems like everyone's poor, no one's got anything worth shit because everyone's waiting on a miracle so everyone'll have jobs again, and everyone'll stop doing heroin and pills, but none of that matters to this little group. They've already got money, and they've always got more than everyone else, and they're just so fucking entitled..."

Rage built in Cassie's voice, and the girl's face reddened. Crash moved her ice cream cone from her right to left hand and reached the free hand over, setting it on Cassie's forearm. Cassie looked down at it, then up at Crash's face. Crash smiled from behind the cone. Cassie's shoulders slumped, and her head dropped and her body shifted forward.

"I guess I'm a little angry," Cassie said.

"That's fine. We're all a little angry sometimes. It's what you do with the anger that counts."

"What do you do?"

Crash pulled her hand back and crunched away more of the chocolate shell. "Eat ice cream. It always helps."

Cassie stirred her Whirlwind again. It had melted to an almost-liquid consistency. She licked the spoon clean then lifted the cup to her mouth and chugged away at the contents. She crunched at the little pieces of Kit Kat, smiling the entire time.

She didn't seem like an angry teenager in that moment but like the little kid she maybe had never had the chance to be.

She dropped the spoon into the empty cup and set it on the dashboard. "What do you want to know about Micki?"

"Whatever you can tell me. How did she meet Billy McCoy?"

"Billy plays guitar in this crappy band that plays at a bar over at the Nightside. You been there?"

The Nightside was in Serenity, nestled between a pawn shop and a tattoo parlor. Crash guessed what they said about real estate was true: the three most important things are location, location, location. A fight or two on a weekend night was inevitable, and Crash had straightened out a few drunken assholes who didn't think she had what it took to put them on their asses.

"How'd she get in there?" Crash said. "It's supposed to be twenty-one and over."

"She gets in there because they don't give a fuck. You give the guy at the door an extra ten bucks, he'll act like that fake ID is real and let you in."

"I'm noting that."

"I figured you would."

"So Micki met Billy one night when the band was playing? What's the band called?"

"The Nightside Regulars. Original, right? They're this shitty cover band, and Micki doesn't even like that crap, but she said Billy was different. Said he wrote his own songs, and she'd heard them and they're good. Said he wants to play rock." She shrugged. "She acts like he'll make it out of Parker County. Like any of us will ever make it out of here."

"You're not stuck here, you know. You can move away, go to college, start another life somewhere."

"Easy for you to say. I ain't got the grades or the money for that shit."

"What do you want to do, then?"

"Most days, nothing. Other days, I wouldn't mind dying,

because it'd mean I can stop having to think about what I'm supposed to do." She wiped at her nose with a Frosty Mart napkin. "I wanna go home now."

"You sure?"

Cassie nodded her head. "Yes, please."

Crash watched the girl. Cassie stared at her hands as though they were separate from her body and liable to take their own action. She knitted her fingers together and looked at her open palms. For a moment, Crash thought she might be praying.

Crash started up the cruiser and shifted it into gear.

Chapter 16

Matt drove by Amy's house and picked up Carl and drove him out to McCluskey Lake. They took Carl's ride, a panel van Amy and Michael had modified for Carl's wheelchair. The motor groaned as it raised Carl and deposited him inside, and Carl could wheel to the front and navigate himself into the passenger seat.

Neither man said much on the drive. When this had started, with Matt taking Carl to the lake, Carl would ask him about cases the department was working. That happened less now. Matt saw the hurt on Carl's face, so he became slower to talk about it. About work, or Crash, or the world that had moved on after the shooting.

What they did now was sit in silence, the bobbers on their lines bouncing in the water. Sometimes there would be a bite, and they'd bring home their catch, and Amy would clean everything up; Rachel refused to have anything to do with it. Amy didn't like that part of things either, but she indulged this nonsense because of Carl, a reward for his willingness to venture out of the house and away from his own solitude.

Matt made a mental note of the mileage on the van's odometer every week. The numbers didn't move from one week to the next often, which meant he was the only one driving the van. It had come off the lot new and set up so Carl could drive, but he always begged off, said he wasn't in the mood. Matt had hit a point of not even asking anymore.

Once they got to the lake, they cruised to the same spot every time, where they could see the sun sink behind the water, the reflection stretching out across the surface, the sky darkening to a deep purple. Matt believed it was the most gorgeous sunset he had ever seen, and he thought that every time he watched it.

The spot was an even and flat concrete platform near a boat launch. Matt supposed it was intended more for kids and old folks. Even with a good cast, it was close to shore, and the traffic of boats being backed in and out of water threw off much chance of catching anything substantial. Still, it was the best spot for Carl's wheelchair, so this was where they came.

Matt felt the weight of the day as he lowered himself into his chair. He had debated calling Carl and canceling. He had even called Rachel and proposed them ordering pizza and watching *The Notebook*, because Rachel loved the damn movie and it guaranteed him getting laid afterward.

"You're fishing with Carl today," she said.

"He'll be okay with not going this week."

"You're fishing with Carl."

"I understand what you're saying, but you keep repeating the same words—"

"I'm not repeating anything; I'm telling you what you're doing. Go fish with Carl. He needs this. You need this. And if you don't smell too much like fish, I'll still fuck you tonight."

Rachel surprised him sometimes.

Carl flipped the lid on his tackle box and snapped open a plastic tub, and Matt caught a whiff of Velveeta.

"That stinks like fuck," Matt said.

Carl smiled as he pulled a small orange chunk and slipped it onto a hook, molding it to fit before he gave the rod a good cast, hitting the button on the reel and letting the hook fly and drop into the water. He reeled in a little and set the cast.

"Every time you say that," Carl said.

"Because it's true every time. That stuff warms up in there

and smells like death when you open it."

"Yet trout love it. And I love trout. So there."

"So there." A beat. "You expecting to catch any trout here?"

"Maybe with the Velveeta. Doubtful, but we've got nothing else to do but try."

Matt took a tub of nightcrawlers from his box. The dirt-filled tub smelled of moist earth, which he preferred over Carl's bait of choice. Matt pulled a worm loose and watched it wiggle between his fingers.

"Do not overthink baiting a hook." Carl's eyes focused on his own line, but the voice pointed in Matt's direction.

"I'm not sure what you're trying to imply, Carl."

"Uh-huh. Put the worm on the goddamn hook."

Matt did, pushing the barbed end through the front of the worm, then again through its middle section, and one last time through the end. The worm continued to struggle and move on the hook.

He threw the cast, letting it drop just shy of Carl's.

The two men sat there without a word exchanged for several minutes before Carl said, "We should have brought beer."

Matt laughed. "Not a good idea on my part."

"Oh yeah. I forget about that."

"Same. I like it when that happens, forgetting the shit you don't want to remember."

"I'll have moments, I'm home and watching a movie and I forget about this goddamn chair. Then I have to empty a piss bag, and nothing drags you back to reality like emptying a piss bag." Carl looked over at Matt. "How's the home invasion stuff going?"

He told Carl about the security video, about the latest incident.

Carl said, "Something smells with that."

"I'm sure it's the Velveeta."

"You'll be laughing out of the other side of your ass when I bring in a nice, fat trout."

"How many sides of ass do you think I've got?"

"Based on what I saw of your ass when you got out of the van earlier, not many, but that's not relevant to the point I'm making about my superior fishing skills. But what stinks is the whole situation you're investigating. How did the number of assailants drop from four to two? Think they're chickening out?"

"Could be. I hope that means someone's getting scared and decides to talk. But the Guthrie job bullshit has me puzzled."

Carl tugged on his line. "You remember that bank holdup? Guthrie National Bank?"

"Yeah. They never caught those guys."

"Nope. Hell of a big deal back then too. Made off with somewhere close to a half-million dollars."

"Wasn't the only job, either. I remember hearing the cops were sure it was the same crew, pulled off three more jobs like that one. Hell, they came back a few weeks later and robbed the same joint again."

Carl nodded. "You gotta admire the balls on that. I know I heard they must have totaled out at more than a million dollars."

Matt adjusted his line. "Goddammit. I hadn't even thought of that being it."

"All I can come up with offhand that would be 'the Guthrie job' since shit doesn't happen in Guthrie County anyway."

"People from Guthrie come to Parker County for excitement."

"Things been a lot more exciting in Parker County of late."

"I doubt that's what they're looking for, excitement-wise."

"I don't judge what people are into. Everyone's got something different that stiffens their dick."

Matt closed his eyes and shook his head. "Phrasing, Carl."

"Hey, I'm not talking about me, obviously." Carl made a noise like he was clearing his throat—when he didn't need to, but he wanted Matt's attention. "While we're on the subject of stiffening dicks, though, Rachel's right. You should put a baby in her."

Matt's head whipped around to throw a stern gaze at Carl.

"That took a sharp and unexpected turn. You and she conspiring on this?"

"We are not. I just agree with her on this."

"How's me getting her pregnant going to help anything?"

"Because the brass tacks of things are this: if you die, she's alone. You don't even know the world of grief that woman will carry on her shoulders. Give her a baby and let her at least have something she can transfer her love and time and affection to when she's gotten done burying you."

"I was leaning toward cremation, not that you care."

"Get shot into space or have a Viking funeral, I don't give a fuck, because this isn't about you, it's about her. Make the situation about you, then you're being a selfish asshole."

"I'm dying. How's that not about me?"

"I'm not talking about you dying; I'm talking about what's left when you're dead."

"And I appreciate the sentiment. So then, as your friend, can I tell you to go back to physical therapy?"

"You can but I doubt I'll listen to you."

"There's a duplicity in you telling me what to do, but you won't listen to my advice."

"Because your advice is pointless, and you're a selfish asshole. Physical therapy won't change my situation."

"You're so sure?"

"Yes, Matt, I am. You want to know how often I hear this from Amy? Every goddamn day. Everyone's got an opinion on what's best for me. Maybe sometime, one of you assholes stops to consider what the fuck I'm dealing with, and that perhaps I have an inkling of what works for me."

"And maybe that's what I'm doing with Rachel and her wanting a baby. Maybe I don't want to leave her with a constant reminder of me whose ass she'll have to wipe and clean up its puke and comfort when the thing cries and send off to school and watch grow up and break her heart a dozen times a day. Maybe the greatest gift I can give her is to die and let her move on with her life, rather than wake up every day with this totem to her dead husband who needs breakfast and clean laundry. What could be the best for you and I both is to stop trying to tell the other one how to live and die, and hope for the best in both cases, whatever the fuck that might be."

Both men sat for a moment.

Carl stared out across the water. A hawk skimmed across the surface, looking for dinner. "Goddamn, but that escalated."

"It did. We might both be assholes."

"We are. That's established fact."

Chapter 17

The Nightside was quiet for a Friday night. The band playing "Gimme Three Steps" was audible down the street as Crash parked. She drove her own vehicle: a 1979 Toyota pickup, faded green and pitted with so much rust it looked as though a heavy rain would disintegrate the thing.

The bouncer at the door was a slab of flab with a shaved head and eyes pushed so far into an oversized face Crash wasn't sure he could see anything. He wore a black T-shirt and shorts and balanced on a stool almost obscured by his mass. He seemed to recognize Crash on sight, even though she was out of uniform in jeans and a plain green T-shirt. He went through the motions of checking her driver's license.

"Nothing going on tonight," he said as he handed Crash back her ID.

"Came to listen to the band."

"I hear 'em three nights a week. They suck."

"Someone said it takes ten thousand hours to master any skill."

"Let 'em spend it somewhere I don't have to listen to them. Wait until you hear what they do to Nickelback."

"Whatever that is, it's bound to be an improvement."

The stage for the band was pushed toward one end of the bar. A banner hanging from the wall behind them proclaimed "The Nightside Regulars." All four members looked old enough to know better than to be playing in a cover band. The lead singer mumbled the lyrics of "Paradise City." The bassist thumped along, looking bored with the entire process. The guitarist had deep intensity cut into his face as he struggled through the song as if trying to remember the chords. The drummer pounded along, throwing in a crash on the cymbals to remind everyone he was there.

A crowd would shuffle in later. Then trouble would start. Crash was grateful to have the night off, if only technically.

Crash ordered a beer. Mandy, the bartender, was a cute blonde, her hair cooked from processing and skin too dark from the tanning bed.

Crash handed her a five. Mandy shook it away.

"House policy is that cops always drink free."

"I like your policy. Be careful of that; I've known cops who could drink you out of business."

Mandy leaned against the counter. She was thin but getting soft, wearing a spaghetti strap tank top that showed off a lack of muscle tone. By contrast, Crash's CrossFit regiment showed off in solid biceps that swelled as she lifted her beer. She'd do extra time to work this off.

"Who you looking for?" Mandy said.

"Who said I'm looking for someone?"

"Never known you to show up unless there was a fight going on, so can't imagine you're coming by to blow off steam."

"You caught me. A guy, he played in the band. Name's Billy McCoy." Crash fished Micki's photo out of her pocket and slid it across the countertop to Mandy. "I think he may be with her."

Mandy glanced at the picture. "I've seen her."

"She's missing. She's seventeen, and her mother's worried about her."

"I'll take your word on that. She comes in and listens to the band. Billy, he played guitar for them until two weeks ago. That's why they've got the new guy playing for them. This new guy, he sounds like he picked his guitar up twenty minutes before he joined."

"The bouncer said they weren't any good."

"They're not, but no one's coming for them, anyway. They like that the beer's cheap."

"The beer's watered down too."

"Yeah, there's that too. It's like that joke about the lady complaining about the restaurant. 'The food's terrible,' she says, 'and the portions are small.'"

The band wrapped up their song, and a few people in the audience set their drinks aside long enough to offer half-hearted applause while everyone else kept on talking and shooting pool and ignoring the band.

The singer said, "Thank you all so much. We're The Nightside Regulars. We'll be taking a short break, and we'll be right back to help you rock on through the rest of the night."

To Crash, it sounded like a threat.

The singer found his way to the bar and motioned to Mandy. "Bud Light."

Mandy pulled a can from the cooler and set it on a napkin in front of him, pulling the tab open. For the singer, the stage persona faded, and what remained was a guy tired and fed up and barely hiding a desire to be elsewhere.

Crash would have called him *skinny-fat*, with a slight build thrown off balance by a bulge rounding out above the belt. He wore ripped jeans that looked like they had earned their distress rather than coming out of the store that way, and a plain black T-shirt stretched too tight over his gut, hanging out untucked. Maybe forty, hairline receding, a healthy amount of gray, and in need of a shave. Not a bad-looking guy if she were in the market for wannabe rockers pushing their bad-idea cover bands into the midst of their midlife crisis. Everyone had a type.

He saw Crash and tipped his beer in her direction. "How you doing tonight, honey?"

"Fantastic. You?"

He shifted himself around to face her better and leaned back a little, digging his elbow into the bar to keep himself upright and hold his balance. "Not bad. How you think we're sounding tonight?"

"Oh, awesome. It's like listening to the real bands."

He smiled and winked at her. "Appreciate that a lot. We put a lot of time into our music. You from around here?"

Crash nodded.

"Haven't seen you in here much."

"I've been here. You must not have noticed me."

"Baby, I'd have noticed you."

Crash pushed back an involuntary gag. "I'm sure all of your groupies get that line, don't they?"

He gave her a dismissive wave. "You might not know it, but I'm a little past the prime to be chasing groupies and teenyboppers. I'm where I'm more appreciative of a woman with more…I suppose you could say life experience."

"How much 'life experience' you wanting with a woman?"

"How much you got?" He made an assessing glance at the distance between them. "Why don't you come down here so I don't feel like I'm yelling?"

Crash hopped off the stool and walked toward him.

He reached his hand out to her. "I'm Kevin."

Crash flipped open her sheriff's ID and pushed her badge out until it was two inches from his face. "Chief Deputy Landing, Parker County Sheriff's Department."

Kevin groaned. "Fuck me running."

"I'll pass, but I appreciate the offer."

Kevin twisted around, putting his back to her. "I'm on break now."

"You are, which means you've got time to talk." Crash hopped up onto the stool next to his. "We can talk about my life experience."

His face soured as his hopes for an easy score spiraled out of control and exploded. He shifted his weight around, away from Crash. "Piss off. I don't have time for cops."

Crash set the photo of Micki on the counter and slid it toward Kevin. "This girl's gone missing. She hung out with your guitarist, Billy McCoy."

Kevin's eyes passed over the picture. "Yeah, she's been around."

"When?"

"I didn't mark it down in my calendar or anything. Two, three months back. She talked to Billy after a gig, and then she was back the next weekend. Then she showed up at practice. It's never a big deal because the guys, they've always got a new piece of ass showing up. You stop learning names after a while."

"Nice attitude."

"I'm realistic, okay? We play Bon Jovi covers; we are not opening up for Metallica." He jabbed at the photo. "She was putting it in Billy's head we needed to do original material, that his stuff was better than what we were hacking out every night."

"You disagreed?"

"Yeah I disagreed, because coming to a dive like this one, listening to a band, you want to sing along, know what shit the band plays. And no one would show up and listen to Billy's prog-rock bullshit." Kevin's shoulders slumped and his body relaxed, and he looked at Crash. "Billy played me samples one night of his originals. It's unformed and rough, but it's also good. King Crimson, or Dream Theater, that kind of vibe. It sure as hell won't draw a crowd in these parts, but if he got his shit together, moved somewhere with an actual scene, he'd make it. Begin with session work, move on from there."

"Micki thought Billy could do better?"

He nodded. "There's always some bitch who's got to show up and be a Yoko Ono."

"The bartender said he stopped playing with you guys."

Kevin looked at Mandy. She'd planted herself on a barstool, staring at her phone, her fingers dancing across the screen.

"Mandy likes to talk, doesn't she?"

Crash tapped her finger on the picture. "This 'bitch,' she's seventeen, and she's disappeared. She shouldn't have been in here to begin with. I can push to shut this joint down for illegal admission of minors, and then there won't be any Nightside for The Nightside Regulars to play, so if I were you, Kevin, I'd worry less about Mandy and more about what you can tell me to help find Billy and find this girl."

Kevin drank more of his beer. "Two weeks ago. Billy didn't show up for practice. I called him, and he said he didn't want to keep playing the same shit every night. She was going off in the background, rooting him on. I said, 'Fuck it, I'm too old for this nonsense,' and told him to have a good fucking life." He cranked his head around to find the guitarist over at the entrance talking to the bouncer. The two men were a sharp contrast from one another. They could have been a comedy team in another time.

"Dave over there, he's lousy, but we didn't have the luxury of time; we needed someone who could learn the songs. I suppose he's done that." He sighed. "He's got to get better. The manager told me he's seeing fewer faces in here the past few weekends, and we're taking those bullets." He sipped at his beer. "Every dream has to die, I guess."

Crash took a notepad and a pen from her back pocket. "I need to know where Billy lives."

Kevin gave her the address. "It's a garage apartment he's renting from someone who owes his family some money."

"You know about his family."

"It's Parker County, honey; everyone knows about the McCoys. You can't buy an ounce of weed around here without them getting something from it. Not that I would ever buy pot, of course."

"Of course not."

The stillness of Serenity at night struck Crash. Even with the deadening thump of The Nightside Regulars playing in the background, the town felt quiet and unmoving, like a dog curled in front of a fire, resting and comfortable.

Not much left to the town. Crash knew the stories, had seen the pictures and been told the history of what the town was like decades before, when the mines had kept half the men employed. Shipped them deep underground, three shifts a day every day to churn out coal. The other half of the men, they worked at the railroad yard, sending the coal out of town, fueling steel mills and power plants, filling the sky with white smoke.

In those days, Serenity had a movie theater—an actual movie house, with a marquee and one screen and a stage that doubled every summer as the site for the Miss Parker County pageant. There were restaurants and stores, and people crowded the streets during the day. Those who remembered those days insisted everything had been better then. People had jobs, and the pizza places were better, and the stores took credit in giant ledgers they kept underneath the counter, and everyone smiled more. To hear the stories, it had to have been a goddamn paradise. And maybe it was. To Crash, it was ancient history.

What Crash knew was this: nothing exists in stasis. The rest of the world wasn't expected to leave Parker County alone. The world never worked like that. What happened was, the coal industry changed. Businesses found cheaper ways to pull coal from the ground. Everything became industrial, and mountaintop removal started, and machines and explosives got to the reserves men couldn't. Jobs dried up. Fewer miners meant less money to spend. Businesses open for generations closed doors, and what replaced the men's wear store and the garage and the toy store and the grocery was one big store outside of town. Nothing rushed into Serenity to fill those empty fronts, and the streets became more and more barren. The trickle of change morphed into a downpour.

Then came the drugs. Mining injuries at first. Seemed anyone with a backache could go to the doctor and get themselves an oxy prescription. Some doctors, they handed out prescriptions like the folks were trick-or-treating. You saw people—people who'd never done shit before that moment—breaking into houses to get at pain pills. Rattle a pill bottle? The Parker County mating call. Lots of blow jobs got exchanged for a few pain pills. Because you could crush them and snort that shit. And the high? Motherfucker, until you've been there and done it, you would not understand.

When the national news decided there was a problem, things changed again. Because that's how change worked: someone in authority noticed, and shit got done. This time the authority was the six o'clock news. Stories about drug addiction in Appalachia. Never saying it right, though. Saying "App-ah-LAY-sha" instead of "App-ah-LATCH-ah." Because you say it the right way, it's how people know where you're from—that you understand. You're a friend if you say it right. You get that iced tea is sweet but corn bread isn't, that chicken and dumplings are a delicacy, and that there's nothing better than watching WVU on a Saturday afternoon. Say it wrong, and you're an outsider—odds were a goddamn Northerner—acting like you could come and fix what's wrong. Nothing set an Appalachian off like an outsider—some do-good grad student or hippie chick earth mama with a liberal arts degree—showing up and saying "Here's what's wrong and here's how to fix it." Nothing wrong that mining coal, a few guns, and going to church on Sunday won't fix.

Nothing got fixed was the problem, Crash figured. She saw the same bullshit, day in, day out. People wanting things to be the way they used to be. Because it had been good for them. Everything else could go to hell. So long as their little patch of grass was green, that was the only thing that mattered. And for Crash, that didn't work. Because there had to be more. There had to be better than just what was good yesterday.

That was on her head when she saw them, the two silhouettes running out from the alleyway across the street, masks pulled over their faces.

Crash reached to her side, gut instinct, for a gun not there. She crossed the street, yelling as she moved. "You! Stop!"

The pair glanced at her. One stopped and stared straight at her and raised a gun into the air.

Crash froze in the middle of the street. It would be a clean shot. Anyone able to handle a gun could plug her dead center in the chest.

They exchanged looks for a few seconds. Crash felt the drumming of her heartbeat, the furious pulsing of blood in her ears. She clenched and unclenched her hands, flexing the fingers. She wished that she had called her mother that morning.

The other masked figure ran back to the one with the gun, grabbed their shirt, and gave an insistent pull. For the length of a heartbeat, Crash thought for sure the person would pull the trigger.

But they didn't. They lowered the gun and dashed to a car, an old-time Mustang with a spoiler and an oversized exhaust. Crash rushed toward it, but the engine growled to life and tires squealed by the time she got there. The license plate had been removed from the rear bracket.

Sweat beaded on her face as she watched the car pop onto two wheels hitting the corner down Wilkerson and disappear into the darkness.

She flipped her attention toward the alleyway. The alley split the difference between a beauty parlor and a florist shop. She thought they had been running away from the florist.

The lock on the side door was busted, the door cracked. She nudged the door open with the toe of her shoe. She paused, thinking she should go back to get a gun and a flashlight.

She heard the hissing noise, smelled gas.

Crash raced out of the alley, calling 911 on her phone as she ran. She was almost to the other side of the street, almost to her truck, when the explosion shattered the florist shop's windows.

The force pushed Crash the final few feet, slamming her body into the hood of her truck. Her cell phone flew from her hand. The heat singed hair on the back of her neck as flames erupted through the broken windows.

She lay in the street, face pressed to the pavement, ears ringing, and didn't move. She wondered what was broken. Thought there had to be something broken. Craned her neck enough to see up the street as a crowd filtered out from the Nightside.

She pushed herself up to an angle and flipped over—motherfucker, but it hurt, and if shit wasn't broken, it goddamn sure wasn't doing great—and watched the flames from the flower shop and listened to the faint sound of the fire department alarm bells way in the distance.

Chapter 18

There are few things as sickeningly sweet as burning flowers, Crash thought as the Serenity Fire Department worked the fire. The department was small—four full-time, and volunteers making up the rest. Both department trucks were there, with a state police cruiser blocking off the street. Serenity had a police department but no one to respond from midnight to 8 a.m., so the state police and the sheriff's department handled those calls. Whatever this was would fall under their jurisdiction. Not that they'd want to deal with it.

All of this as Crash leaned against her truck, the blaze barely in the distance. The paramedics offered to transport her to Parker General, and she declined. Nothing broken, she figured, though she was sore already and knew it would be worse in the morning. There was bruising across her lower torso along her stomach. Probably a cracked rib too. She pondered whether she should have taken the paramedics' offer. Wasn't exactly her first cracked rib, though, and if nothing else, she could wrap it herself when she got home.

Not that she would say anything to Matt as he leaned next to her, his arms folded across his chest. The heat from the fire stretched across the street to them. For Matt, it was probably pleasant. He stayed colder than usual.

"How you feeling?" Matt said.

"Been better." She pressed her hand against the back of her

head. "Singed some of my hair."

"Did you get a look at them?"

"Got a look at two people in masks."

"Not four?"

"Not four."

"There seems no shortage of late of people running around, all hours of the night, wearing masks."

Crash twisted her torso around from one side to the other.

"You're going to hurt yourself," Matt said.

"Already been blown up tonight, so I'm not sure how doing this is going to make things worse." She bent at the waist and tried to touch her toes. A sharp pain shot through her. She seized up, everything tightening. She leaned back against the pickup.

Matt said, "You should go to the hospital."

"I'm fine. Just sore. I'll take Tylenol."

"I tried that too. Turned out I had cancer."

"It's a thick, heavy line between getting blown up and having cancer, but thanks for the concern." She watched the fire. "Think it's the same people who attacked the Campbells and the Carltons?"

"No reason to think it's not the same people. No reason they'd blow up the florist shop, either."

"We're short on reasons they beat up two different pairs of old people."

Matt nodded. He pointed to the burning building.

"You know what this is?" he said.

"What?"

"A message. That they're done dicking around. They mean business."

"What they did before wasn't what I'd call 'dicking around.' They put old people in the hospital."

"I'm not saying that their gauge is properly set; I'm just saying this is an escalation tactic." He glanced over at her. The light from the flames showed light purple on her face. The firefighters were getting the blaze under control. "You sure you're okay?"

"I'm pissed. They pulled a gun on me."

"Did you identify as a police officer?"

"I didn't. Didn't show ID or a weapon. Wouldn't have done any good."

"Think they'd have shot you?"

"They had me right there. They could have shot me."

"A good thing they didn't."

"I suppose that's where I should be thankful for the small things."

"One should always be grateful for not getting shot. That's a damn fine day right there."

"What do we do now?"

"Well, after watching the flower shop burn up, going home and taking allergy medicine seems like a good idea."

"It's always surprising when Benadryl gets used for its intended purposes around here."

"How cynical of you, Crash."

"I'm a person who's spent a crazy amount of time busting meth labs, Matt. *Cynical* and *realistic* are synonyms sometimes."

At the end of the street, near one of the trooper roadblocks, a car pulled up and Matt and Crash watched as a man in shorts and a polo shirt got out. Matt would have guessed him somewhere well into midlife, with skinny arms and legs and a round gut and a gray mustache pushed onto a thin, drawn face. He talked to the state troopers, peering over their shoulders and staring at the fire, shaking his head. The flames reflected in the wetness on his face.

Matt tapped Crash on the shoulder and they walked over. Matt introduced himself and Crash.

The man shook Matt's hand. "I'm David Winthrop. That was my flower shop." He sniffed and blew his nose into a handkerchief. "That's my fucking life there, Sheriff."

"I'm sorry about this, Mr. Winthrop," Matt said. "Any idea who would do this to you?"

Confusion crossed Winthrop's face. "What do you mean? You mean it's not an accident. Someone said it was a gas leak."

Crash said, "I confronted a pair of individuals running away from your shop just before the explosion. We suspect they're the ones responsible for causing the fire."

"I'm at a loss about that. I'm a fucking florist, for Christ's sake. I make wedding bouquets. We donate all the flowers to the high school for homecoming every year. There's nothing I do that would cause someone to do something like this."

"Is there an off chance you know Gary Campbell or Peter Carlton?"

"Sure. I see them at Chamber of Commerce meetings, and they tried to get me to join this group a couple years ago, when I bought the shop."

"Was it the Benevolent Order of the Everlasting Knights?"

"That sounds right. It seemed like bullshit, a bunch of old guys wanting to keep the thing alive."

"When did you buy the shop?" Crash said.

"Nine or ten years ago. Bought it from Frank Dodson before he retired and moved down to Florida. Gary and Peter, they said Frank had belonged to the Order and felt like it'd be nice to carry the tradition."

"You didn't join?" Crash said.

Winthrop's smile pushed the mustache out across his face. "I'm not the fraternal organization type. It didn't seem like my thing."

Matt nodded. "You kept the shop's old name, though."

"Shop's been here for decades. Made no sense to come in, change all of that. People came and bought flowers, so who cared what I called the place." Winthrop glanced up and down the street. "Was anyone hurt?"

Crash said, "No. Is there any chance you've gotten any unusual communications in the past few days? Weird phone calls? Strange letters?"

Winthrop held up a finger. "Hold that thought for a moment."

He rushed back to his car and opened the rear driver's side door, bending over and looking around the back seat. Matt and Crash traded looks with one another, and Crash shrugged.

Winthrop popped back out of the car, holding a manila envelope. He walked back and handed it to Matt. "I got that yesterday. Was slid through the mail slot on the shop door."

The envelope was blank. No address, no stamp, no marking of any kind. Matt flipped it around and drew out a folded sheet of paper.

"At first, I thought it was some kind of joke," Winthrop said. "People do weird stuff all the time. Could have been a promotion for a business opening in town. Who knows? But I checked around and no one else had gotten anything like this."

It looked like a ransom note from a movie, the words constructed from cutouts from magazines and newspapers. It read, "We want what's ours. We want the Guthrie money."

Chapter 19

Matt was already up when Rachel stirred. By the time he came home, showered, and got to bed, he was still too wired to sleep, and instead he tossed and turned most of the night. He was sure he had kept Rachel awake along with him. She was a light sleeper but too polite to ever admit his insomnia affected her.

He felt groggy, and his body ached as he made himself coffee and went to sit on the back deck. This time of day, on a Saturday, the neighborhood was quiet, with the early-morning crickets chirping and the grass wet with dew. It was warm already, and Matt suspected summer would be brutal. The dew would turn into humidity, and the air would get heavy and wet, and the oppressive nature would weigh him down with every breath he took.

This wasn't some new thing, either—something that had just come from global warming. Matt remembered most of his summers this way, where the air always felt like it was teetering on the brink of a storm, where standing outside and doing nothing could still reduce clothes to wet rags in a matter of minutes. It made him want to do nothing more than sit inside with the air conditioning running full blast.

A lawn mower started down the street. Matt gave his own lawn an appraising gaze. It could probably do with a mow. Not that he could do it. He couldn't imagine pushing the mower through, front yard and back. Thinking about it made him tired. Maybe he could hire one of the neighborhood kids to do it.

That thought seemed worse somehow. Because then it became the acknowledgment that he wasn't who he used to be. It wasn't the simple act of getting older. It was that he was dying. Dying faster than the people around him. Several summers back, when it had been just him, when he had been drinking too much and staring at the blank walls and hating himself, when he had gone out and wrestled his ancient lawn mower into submission, priming the engine and yanking the cord, and it finally stirred to life in an oily blue haze. He pushed it around, shearing the grass down to a level just above the soil. He hated mowing the grass. Hated it with a passion. Did it only because the last thing he needed was the neighbors talking shit about him, going on that the sheriff didn't take care of his lawn.

And here he was, back with Rachel, and he couldn't do it. That most basic of husbandry chores. Another brick slid into the invisible wall between him and the rest of the world. The living, breathing world. The divide, greater, taller, wider, with every passing day. But what hurt worse than anything—the cut that slit the door—was knowing there wasn't a goddamn thing he could do about it. All he had left was this. Just working to move forward. Keep being a good cop. Try to keep anyone else from getting hurt. Hope that it wasn't too much for Rachel when he was gone.

He heard the door open and her footsteps coming up behind him. She tried to be stealthy, but she lacked that gift. He smiled at the thought of her sneaking up on him, on her tiptoes, ever so sure she was getting one on him.

Rachel set a cup of coffee down on the table next to Matt, then rested her head on top of his head and wrapped her arms around his chest. He took hold of her hands and held them there.

"Did I scare you?" Rachel said.

"Terrified me. I'm stunned the heart attack didn't do me in."

She kissed his head and came around, taking the chair next to him. "How bad was this thing last night?"

"I hope you don't have any floral arrangements ordered for the near future. Outside of what you're planning for the funeral."

She shook her head. It was the slightest hint of movement, really, and the unobservant eye might not have noticed it, but Matt, through the years, he had learned her behaviors, trained to pick them up.

"Not today, honey," she said. "I don't need this today."

He took her hand. "Sorry."

"It's okay."

Matt talked to her about the fire. She listened the way she always did, with small nods and the occasional "uh-huh" or a question to clarify something. The times when no one was hurt, she was more attentive, more acknowledging. When there was something with serious injuries, with fatalities, those were harder for her, and the listening became more passive. Matt knew it wasn't that Rachel didn't care; it was that she couldn't handle it. Even after all these years, Rachel struggled to process the human capacity to harm one another.

The doorbell rang. They each glanced at the front door, then one another.

"Did you invite someone over for brunch?" Matt said.

"Not anyone we like."

Matt pushed himself out of the chair and answered the door. It was Crash. She wore a Dead Kennedys T-shirt and blue jeans and held a to-go cup of coffee in one hand and had a messenger bag slung over her shoulder. Matt realized he had never seen Crash carry a purse.

Crash said, "I spent the morning looking into Frank Dodson. Plus, the surveillance video from Campbell's place got dropped off at the office this morning. I thought you might want to see it."

Matt looked at Crash through the screen door. "Good morning, Crash."

She smiled. "Morning, Sheriff."

"It's Saturday morning, Crash."

"Yes, it is."

Crash blinked. She looked at him with an utter lack of guile. There were times Matt felt like he was dealing with a little kid, one who couldn't tell a lie, who couldn't pick up on social cues. She would have been the one who showed up at a neighbor's house at eight in the morning, first day after moving in, asking if they had kids who wanted to come outside to play.

Matt let her in and led her to the back deck. Rachel lifted her eyebrows as they came through the door, then turned on a functional smile and sipped her cup of coffee.

"How are you this morning, Crash?" Rachel said.

Crash pulled out a chair and sat at the table. "Wide awake and excited about life."

"Wonderful." Rachel's gaze turned to Matt. "It's Saturday, Matt."

Matt nodded. "Yes, it is."

Rachel gave a small exhale. "Should I make brunch then?"

"I think we're good, honey. I might make myself a couple of eggs in a bit. I'm not sure if Crash is hungry."

Crash began to empty the contents of her messenger bag onto the table. "I ate before I came over," she said as she opened a laptop.

"Must have been awfully early," Rachel said.

"It was." Next came some paperwork and a DVD jewel case.

Rachel exhaled again. "I'll go find things to do while you crime busters bust crime and whatnot."

She rose to her feet, coffee cup in hand, and headed for the door. Matt reached out and took her by the waist and pulled her toward him, his eyes meeting hers. Her smile remained faint and elusive. She kissed him lightly, their lips brushing against one another.

"You kids have fun now." She pulled herself loose and went inside.

Matt took the chair next to Crash. She furrowed her brow. "I don't feel like Rachel likes me much."

"It's Saturday, Crash."

Crash looked at Matt like a puppy, not sure what she had done wrong.

Matt shook his head. "Let's get started."

Chapter 20

Matt glanced at the DVD in its plain plastic jewel case. The DVD had the Tri-Comm emblem stickered onto it, but otherwise, the envelope was empty. "No note or anything. Not even something from the attorney."

"I didn't make the best of impressions when I delivered the court order."

"Turned on all the charm?"

"Man was an asshole. Wanted to give me shit."

"That's something to expect out there, Crash."

"Doesn't mean I have to tolerate it. I don't wear a badge because it brings out the color in my eyes."

"But it does."

Crash set the disk inside the computer's DVD drive and twisted the laptop around so they both could watch the screen.

The video was black and white and grainy, split into four quadrants: the front yard of the Campbell house, the backyard, the garage entrance, and a side view of the house.

"How much footage is there?" Crash said.

"The court order asked for from the time the Campbells said they left for that night, leading up to when Tim arrives on the scene. To be sure we got when the suspects broke in."

Crash leaned in close to the monitor, squinting. "That's five hours."

"You've got somewhere else to be?"

"We can fast forward past this stuff and get to where someone is actually breaking in."

"You must be a terrible movie date."

"Hush, or I won't buy you any popcorn."

Crash fast-forwarded through the video until two figures appeared in the quadrant covering the backyard. Both wore Halloween masks over their faces. One mask was of a long-faced man with a mustache, and the other was of a white-faced woman, pink cheeks and red lips painted into a bow.

"The one is wearing a Guy Fawkes mask," Crash said. "*V for Vendetta* bullshit. That other one, the baby doll—looking one, that's like the one the chick wears in *The Purge*."

"What the fuck is *The Purge*?"

"It's a horror movie. Haven't you seen it?"

"I've not. I'll bet I'm not missing out on much, either."

"It's political bullshit, but it's okay."

"These look like the folks from last night?"

"Body-wise, yes. They weren't wearing those same masks, but build and everything matches."

Both wore black, both wore gloves. Guy Fawkes carried a crowbar, and Baby Doll a baseball bat. The bat used to kill the Carltons' dog. *Coming ready*, Matt thought. Not just about violence or causing chaos. With these assholes, there was an intent.

Matt moved the footage ahead, almost frame by frame, as Guy Fawkes whacked at the doorknob with the crowbar over and over until it fell off. Guy Fawkes pushed the door open with one finger, then looked at Baby Doll. They gave one another a nod and walked inside.

"So now they go and deactivate the alarm," Matt said.

"We still don't know how they knew the code, though."

"When we catch them, we can ask them."

"That's a huge vote of confidence toward our collective sleuthing abilities, but if we figure out how he got the code, it might lean us toward catching him."

"That's one way of handling it, sure."

"How about the daughter?"

Matt drank some coffee. "Iris? No way. I suppose Mrs. Campbell might have told her, but that's depending on Mr. Campbell having even told the code to her."

"He doesn't seem the kind to trust a woman with something important like a security code. Or car keys. Or a credit card. Or anything else. Ever."

"An old man with old-school thinking, Crash."

"What about a Tri-Comm employee?"

"That would be the most logical. I can talk to Doug Jones, get a list of employees and see what dots connect. Unless you'd like to take another swing at the plate."

"I'm not on Mr. Jones's Christmas card list. That ball can rest in your court."

The time code on the video was stamped for 7:10 p.m. The Campbells had gotten home after ten. That meant Guy Fawkes and Baby Doll had almost three hours in the Campbell house.

"This must be when the two of them were inside redecorating the place with shit and piss," Crash said.

"The two of them," Matt said. "Where's the other two?"

"That's what I'm wondering myself."

"Campbell was very definite on there having been four people. So he was in shock and lost track of numbers during everything—"

"Or he flat-out fucking lied to us."

"I'm leaning more toward the former than the latter."

"For a man who got beaten and whose wife got put in a coma, he's been unhelpful as hell."

On the video, Guy Fawkes and Baby Doll reappeared, coming out the back door. Matt paused the video and stared at the image on the screen.

Guy Fawkes was tall and wiry. Baby Doll was shorter, boyishly constructed—similar to Crash—but no denying the person was female.

Matt tapped his middle finger against the laptop. "Campbell's hiding shit. And I don't like being lied to."

"You may have chosen the wrong career path, then."

Matt told Crash about his conversation with Carl and the discussion about Carl's theory around the Guthrie job.

"Four bank robberies, and they netted more than a million bucks, and no one ever got caught?"

"Nope. It was the cleanest of getaways ever. Except for the woman they killed."

The first robbery had been as perfect of a bank heist as one could have hoped for—something that would have been the pride of a Hollywood movie. Nine thirty on a Monday morning. The Guthrie National Bank—the largest bank in three counties—almost busted at the seams with cash from the weekend night deposits, money dropped in by businesses from the nearby Guthrie Mall and shopping plazas.

The lobby was active but not full when the car pulled up outside and three men ran in. Fast and coordinated. Knocked out the security guard at the entrance first then moved their way throughout the bank. Ski masks and military-grade assault weapons. They said only the bare minimum, ordering everyone to the ground, and had the tellers empty their drawers. Took IDs from the tellers and threatened to kill anyone who put an exploding dye packet into a bag.

In and out, four minutes, plenty of time before the state police got there.

First haul: half a million.

It was a hell of a big deal when the Feds showed up—elbowing in for space where state police, county, local cops—everyone with tin pressed into a badge, it seemed. The Feds found what everyone else found.

Which was nothing.

No suspects. No leads. No clues. Nothing. An operation as slick as buttered shit down a warm tin roof. Only trace of anything was the getaway car—a Ford Escort stolen two counties over, left abandoned in a Walmart parking lot. No fingerprints.

A professional crew, the Feds determined. Organized crime, maybe out of Pittsburgh or Chicago. Come down into the sticks and take out easy targets for fast cash. Expect to see more of these, they said.

Two weeks passed. Nothing. Things settled down.

Then the crew showed back up. On a Tuesday. Just to shake things up.

As smooth as the first. Took out the guard. Worked through the customers, cleaning out wallets and purses, any cash deposits they might have planned on making that day never going into the accounts.

Another threat to the tellers, warning them off the dye packs.

Except there was a new girl working. Tina Miller. Three weeks in. Had been off the day of the first robbery because her kid had come down with a stomach bug. This girl, twenty-three. The stories the newspapers wrote about her afterward, she sang the first alto in her church choir. Volunteered at her son's preschool. "Sweetest young woman ever," was what several people said.

The teller next to her saw Tina slip the dye pack into the bag. Didn't get to say anything. The barrel off a sawed-off shotgun was so close to her head, she smelled gun oil.

The gunman behind the counter—the one watching everything—he noticed Tina and the dye pack as well.

And he shot her.

The screaming and chaos that followed the gunshot helped the gunmen escape. It was the moment where everyone in the bank found out getting shot wasn't like in the movies. The gunshot cut through Tina s'chest and pierced a lung. She flew backward off her stool like she'd been struck by a car and slammed into the cold white tile. Her heart kept pumping, blood flowing into her lung, and she coughed up red streams. Crying the entire time, her eyes never moving from the photo of her children on her workspace. She took a few minutes to die, to choke on her own blood. She was gone before the ambulance sirens had even gotten close.

The Feds danced their way in again and doubled their efforts this time. Because you rob a bank, there's a federal crime. But murder someone during the commission of a federal crime, that'll put you in the gas chamber.

The town held candlelight vigils for Tina, and churches raised money to help with her funeral expenses, and someone started a trust fund for her son for college. Her husband, John Miller, was a miner, a nice-enough guy who found himself thrust into attention he didn't want, a widower at twenty-four. He told one of the morning news shows, through tears streaking down his face, that he hoped the person who'd killed his wife burned in hell for the rest of eternity.

And then again, just like that, nothing. The FBI, the local police—no one found shit. No one could explain it, either. Most bank robberies were low-return affairs, and the folks who committed them almost always got caught. But these guys, this was like something out of a movie. A magazine referred to the crime as "a hillbilly version of *Heat*," the DeNiro-Pacino heist flick. West Virginia politicians didn't take to the comment kindly and went on a multi-day tirade about it before the magazine issued an apology.

"So whoever attacked Carlton thinks he had something to do with the Guthrie bank robberies?"

"And Campbell and Dodson." Matt shrugged. "The first question is did Campbell? Since whoever broke into his house and beat him senseless was convinced he did. We can prove a connection for Campbell, Carlton, and Dodson through the Everlasting Knights. And no matter what Campbell says, I'd bet you five bucks his attackers are the same people from the Carlton attack and the duo from last night."

Crash patted the papers on the table. "Once I got home last night, I did a little research on Dodson."

"Color me surprised. What did you find out?"

Crash flipped through the papers on the table. "Dodson sold the flower shop to Winthrop nine years ago, did the whole 'snowbird' thing and migrated down to Florida. He'd owned the shop for about thirty years prior, him and his wife. Winthrop was right about the Chamber of Commerce and the Everlasting Knights. Dodson was eyeball-deep into both."

"What's he up to now?"

"In the most realistic terms, he's down to about six feet below. Complications from a stroke three years ago."

"But whoever set off that explosion last night, they didn't know that. They thought Dodson still owned the shop." Matt ran a hand across the back of his neck, twisting his head around, searching for the cracking noise. The weariness swept over him like an avalanche.

"What now?" Crash said.

"I'll talk to Campbell," Matt said. "Anything new on Carlton?"

"I called this morning. Nothing's changed."

Matt stood and stretched. Things popped and cracked that he wasn't sure were supposed to make those noises, and he felt like he sounded like wax paper. He blew out a long, deep breath and smiled at Crash a big, goofy grin.

"Let's go fight crime," he said.

Through the glass door, Crash saw Rachel moving back and forth in the kitchen, trying to look like she wasn't watching when she was.

"She won't be happy," Crash said.

"She won't, but she'll be okay today."

"What about tomorrow?"

"I'll deal with that tomorrow. Hell, I might be dead by then."

Crash repacked everything into her messenger bag. "Aren't

you people supposed to stay positive and shit?"
"Sure. Whatever."

Chapter 21

Matt drove over to Gary Campbell's house and knocked and waited. No answer. He checked around outside the house and saw nothing that showed any kind of activity. He peeked into the garage. It was empty.

He scribbled out a note on the back of a business card, asking Campbell to call him at his first opportunity, and circled his cell phone number for emphasis before he wedged it in the crack between the door and the frame.

In his car, he reached for his wallet and rifled through it for a moment until he found the business card Iris Warner had given him, then called her.

She answered on the third ring. "Hello?"

"Ms. Warner, this is Sheriff Simms. How are you today?"

"Whenever the police call, it's safe to presume things could be better."

"Maybe I'm calling to tell you, you won our annual potluck dinner raffle."

"Did I?"

"Depends on if you attended the potluck dinner and bought tickets."

"I did not."

"Then most likely, you didn't win. But I'd like to talk to you if you have a few moments."

"Being in Parker County means you've got nothing but time,

I've noticed." She told him her hotel and gave him the room number. He said he would be on over.

The Wiltshire was the closest that Parker County had to a hotel. Everything else was chain motels that sprung up in the aftermath of the ATV trails the county set up two decades prior. Those were built on reclaimed surface mining sites, the intent being to charge people a premium to tear through the mountains on four-wheelers. The motels intended to give them a place to rest before going at it again the next day. Someone somewhere saw all of this as an investment in the state, a way to boost tourism and bring out-of-area cash into the community, and it had, but it wasn't a constant stream of revenue and nowhere near enough to balance the revenue lost once coal collapsed.

The Wiltshire had been something to see decades before when Serenity had been—as the sign on the city limits proclaimed—"the heartbeat of the American coal industry." Crystal chandeliers had hung from the lobby ceiling. The tile floors had gleamed like diamonds. During the Prohibition, bootleggers kept the bar stocked with illegal booze, and the sounds of Chicago jazz pressed against the inside walls, threatening to shake the stones loose.

Parties at the Wiltshire were the stuff of legends. It had been where the monied few of Parker County went to escape the resounding poverty that encroached on their idyllic little chunk of the American Dream. Coal barons, railroad operators, timber kings—hell, even the family that owned the *Parker County Herald-Tribune*—came to celebrate that they were surviving and thriving while the rest of the world stood in lines for soup. They listened to jazz music performed by black musicians who couldn't even spend a night in the hotel. The owners brought in a French chef from Paris who maintained an open-all-hours policy in the kitchen, serving at the whims of drunken guests at three in the morning.

Time caught up with everyone, though, and as fortunes faded, so did the glamor of the Wiltshire. Chandeliers came down. The swing and jump jazz that had filled the halls became the country radio station broadcast from two doors down. Veal and lamb disappeared from the restaurant menu, and eventually the restaurant itself closed. By the times that Matt remembered, the Wiltshire had become a stop station for railroaders, somewhere to sleep until they caught the next train back home. The glories and glamor of long-ago times faded and left nothing behind but the faintest hint there had once been something great.

Matt's shoes clicked against the marble lobby floor. The tile was worn and needed cleaned. The furniture, threadbare and faded and thin in patches, showed the stuffing underneath. The elevator trembled on the ride to the fourth floor. Upstairs, the hallway was narrow and confining, and he half expected to see a pair of creepy twins at the other end. The carpet had been red once—vibrant and deep and the color of fresh blood—but had faded now to something almost pink, or "salmon," Rachel might have said. Matt wasn't sure what the difference would have been, but he knew that Rachel would.

Iris opened the hotel door after Matt's knock. Dressed in a plain white T-shirt that somehow looked expensive, and blue jeans. Her face was blank and impassive when she saw Matt, and she stepped aside and motioned him into the room.

It was a suite with a small living room area with a couch and a love seat and a coffee table, and the bedroom next to it. A laptop was open on the coffee table next to a cup of coffee with thin tendrils of steam rising from it. Matt eyed the coffee with a desire he normally saved for Rachel, or women like Iris Warner. It was a moment where he pondered what had happened to his priorities.

"Can I interest you in a cup, Sheriff?" Iris said. She gestured to a coffee maker resting on a counter.

"Please. Black."

Iris filled a cup—an actual stoneware mug—from the pot

and handed it to Matt. He nodded his thanks and sat down on the love seat. Iris sat across from him on the couch.

"I always bring a coffee pot with me," she said, reaching for her own cup. "Hotels have gotten terrible about coffee, and I believe it to be a thing that most separates us from other members of the animal kingdom."

"Agreed. The ability to use tools and to use those tools to pour hot water over ground coffee beans. I know a guy—not a friend, per se—who has the same peccadilloes about coffee as you. Perhaps I should introduce the two of you."

Iris smiled and sipped from her cup. "Is matchmaking part of the sheriff's job around here?"

"Oh, I wouldn't recommend dating this guy. He's a jerk. He just has a litany of coffee issues." Matt leaned back in the couch. The furniture hadn't been in style in decades, and the wear was apparent, and he felt the nudge of springs underneath his ass poking through the cushions.

"What can I do for you today, Sheriff?" Iris said. "I heard the explosion last night. I thought we were under attack, and then I wondered who the hell would attack here."

"We haven't had a good earth-shattering kaboom in a few years. Someone blew up the flower shop."

"Someone set off a bomb in Serenity?"

"Nothing so technical. It appears they ignited a natural gas line to the furnace."

"That seems…random."

"And yet, it is unlikely to be random."

"You have to have a fair amount of intent to blow up a florist." Iris sipped her coffee. "Your little department has a lot of balls in the air. How do you manage?"

"We plug away, and we drink plenty of coffee."

Iris smiled. "I like you, Sheriff. You seem to be one of the better people left in this hellhole."

"I'm rather fond of this hellhole. I work hard to keep it safe."

"I meant no offense, Sheriff. I grew up here. But I'm someone who knows mountains get confused with walls, and they end up being barriers that not only keep people in, but they keep ideas out. It's why I ran as far and as fast as possible, the first chance I had."

"Escape seems to have suited you."

"I've made a life that's mine, that no one else can lay claim to. There's something to be said for building something that doesn't have another person's name attached to it. Family and names, that's half of what drives this place. You grow up, people ask you, 'Who's your family? Who's your parents? Oh, you're so-and-so's little brother, or little sister, or third cousin twice removed.' It doesn't give you much chance to have autonomy." She drank more coffee. "My last name was Campbell. My father owned a chain of grocery stores called Campbell's Market. That's hard to escape."

"Worse legacies to have."

"Not when everyone around you is poor and they assume you're rich because your last name is on signs and billboards. Don't misunderstand me; my family had money. We had satellite TV in 1982, so I was watching MTV when other kids weren't even sure what it was. We bought a new car every three years, and we took two weeks every summer to go to Myrtle Beach. Money earns you friends for a while, but it also gets you a lot of resentment you can't do anything about, because you're a kid and that shit is out of your control. And when business declined, that became the headache of watching my parents working to keep up appearances while trying to make sure the lights stayed on."

"Was that about the time Walmart came to town?"

"Yes. You had a gleaming, twenty-four-hour grocery store option, this limitless set of choices, and there was no way to compete with that. If I had the capacity to muster something resembling sympathy for my father, I would have felt bad for him because he busted his ass to keep things going, but the tide turned against him. He tried to compete, but customer loyalty only goes so far, and then you choose between loyalty to a grocery store and affording to feed your kids."

Matt nodded. "Was your father friends with a man, name of Peter Carlton?"

Iris seemed to let the name wander through her mind. "There was a Carlton who Gary did business with. Worked at a bottling company?" The last part, she said toward Matt as though seeking confirmation of the fact.

"That would be him."

"I think he and the old man, they may have been in one of those groups old white guys like to join. The Eternal Brotherhood of the Sleepless Knights—that kind of bullshit."

"Did Carlton come around much?"

"Some. It was a long time ago, Sheriff. I'm not sure why you're asking me these things and not him. Or is the old man still being difficult?"

"He wasn't what you'd term *enthusiastic* about talking before, and I doubt he'll be chattier now."

"This Peter Carlton, he was attacked, wasn't he?" She leaned forward, resting her elbows on her knees, putting her hands together. "You think my parents and the Carltons were picked for a reason?"

"I can't say. What I know is that we don't have much, so anything we find out, it's more than there was before."

"You should write fortune cookies with dialogue like that."

"I practice in front of the mirror at home." Matt's coffee had cooled, and now it tasted bitter. He set the cup aside. "Mind if I ask you a personal question?"

"It's your job, so you'll ask it anyway, and I suppose you asking permission is your way of being polite."

"Why don't you and your father speak?"

Iris smiled, but any hint of warmth or humor dissipated behind her eyes. "I caught my father cheating on my mother. It wasn't long before he closed up the stores. I came home from college—

it was a surprise visit, and I hadn't warned them ahead of time the way I normally did—and I walked through the front door and I heard my father on the phone. He was telling someone he'd be over later that night, and he said something about his wife not knowing, that he wouldn't risk her finding out. It short-circuited something in my head, and I turned and left.

"I drove around for a while, and when it got dark, I parked away from the house but where I could watch the driveway. About nine that night, he pulled his car out, and I followed him to some white trash trailer park in the boondocks. He—" The words turned sharp, and she had to choke out what followed. "This pregnant bitch walked out and hugged him." Iris tried to keep her face hard and cold. "She hugged him, kissed him on the cheek, and they went on inside. That's when I put the pieces together. My father, the motherfucking asshole, had gotten this cunt *pregnant*."

She blew out an angry sigh. "My mother is not perfect, but she's better than that asshole deserved. I debated how to tell her, then decided not to. It wasn't my duty as a daughter to destroy her world that way. So over time, I carved my father out of my world. For years he'd ask me why I was doing this to him. He pleaded with me to tell him what was going on, and every time I said the same thing, that he knew the reason. After a while, he stopped asking."

She glanced toward the windows. Dark clouds showed in the distance, and Matt thought he heard a rumble of thunder.

"The children in the pictures in my parents' living room, those are children from my mother's side of the family. My parents had to make do with those substitutions because I've never given them grandchildren. Do you know why, Sheriff?"

"I wouldn't venture a guess."

"Because the greatest harm I could offer my father was to deny him another person to lie to whenever he told them 'I love you.' I'm sure whatever little bastard offspring he has running around might give him a grandchild someday—the shit stain is well into breeding years by now—but I chose to deny him one he could claim in public. When something happens to my mother, at her funeral, once she is in the ground and he believes the pain can't be worse, I will stand there next to the gravesite and I will explain to him why I've not spoken to him for all these years. And I will walk away from him and everything in his world with him knowing his betrayal of my mother sealed this fate of him dying alone."

She turned back to Matt and flashed that empty smile again.

Matt stood. "Thank you for your time, Ms. Warner. I'll let myself out."

Matt's hand was on the doorknob when he stopped and looked back at Iris. Her attention was back to the windows, though he felt as though there was nothing going on outside she could see. Those windows just showed a time two decades old and the hurt accumulated since then.

"Ms. Warner?"

She remained turned away. "Yes?"

"How's your mother doing?"

There was a pause. "She's going to die, Sheriff. What the people did to her, the damage was too much for a woman her age. The doctors don't expect her to wake up, so the question becomes if the old man has enough guts to do what needs done. Based on his prior experience, I'm not holding my breath."

Matt let those words hang then walked out.

With the door closed behind him, the air in the hallway felt cooler and more free to Matt, and he took in deep breaths on his way to the elevator.

Chapter 22

Billy McCoy's apartment sat over the garage of a split-level in a planned community that hadn't gone according to plan. The sign at the outset read "Waterview Gardens," which made Crash laugh since the only nearby water to have a view of was the Tomahawk River, and it was little more than a narrow strip of brown water trickling along to a better stream. The Tomahawk was shallow and slow, and the only time it caused an issue was during heavy rains, which threw debris in and blocked up the flow, backing up the water and spilling it out onto its banks. It didn't seem worth paying money for the view.

Not that many people did that at Waterview Gardens. Five or six houses were finished and families lived there, but the others were frozen in a half-completed state. Crash's guess was the houses had been like that for a while. She had seen this in other places, where someone got the bright idea to construct a housing community but ran out of money before it was finished. Maybe it wasn't the best idea to build overpriced houses somewhere no one could afford them, Crash thought. Maybe that was too much common sense, and that was why she wasn't in real estate.

The lady who answered the door looked at Crash with caution shoved behind an overwrought smile. The model of a middle-class housewife, in yoga pants and a WVU T-shirt. A TV blared in the background, and from it a children's show played something involving intergalactic warriors.

Crash told her she understood Billy lived in an apartment above the garage, and that she needed to check it out. The wife said Billy hadn't been there in about a week, that he had said nothing to them about leaving; he had just vanished.

"My husband told Billy he could stay here," the wife said as she unlocked the apartment door. "I didn't like it, but Jake kept telling me what a good guy Billy was and how he needed somewhere to be for a while. Didn't tell me much beyond that. I always kept all the doors locked, though. Got to be careful, right?" She paused, key in the lock, and said, "Billy's not involved in anything, is he? Because I will beat Jake if he brought a criminal into my home and—"

"Nothing like that at all. It's where he's missing. There might be a clue here somewhere." Crash wanted to keep the peace between Jake and his wife. Last thing she needed was to find herself out here tonight breaking up a domestic.

Crash stepped into the apartment. Nothing but a studio with a bathroom at the far end, so not much to see, but then again, Billy likely didn't need much. Crash said thanks to the wife and that she'd lock up and let her know when she left.

Crash snapped on latex gloves and started her search. The place stunk of weed. Crash figured Billy smoked a lot and didn't open the windows much. Didn't want the neighbors finding out. No bed, but a Walmart futon was pushed against the wall. Decorations were limited to posters fastened by Scotch tape. Crash recognized some of the movies—stoner comedies. Not shocking, all things considered. Other posters were of bands Crash had never heard of. The bands all looked like a variety of angry white guys striking the same poses as a thousand bands before them.

Collaged together onto a corkboard were photos all done with an unmistakable feminine touch. Hearts and ribbons and girly shit that Crash didn't get. She recognized Micki Miller. Took a minute, though, because what was here wasn't the angry Micki in her pictures. This Micki wore an honest, unguarded smile. There was a joy she couldn't hide.

With her in some of the photos was Billy McCoy: a decent-enough-looking guy, with longish hair and narrow features and earrings lining up his left ear. He didn't smile much and looked more bothered by the picture-taking process. In some he would glance over at Micki, and there'd be a flicker of a smile. Too busy being a tough guy.

An end table next to the futon was stacked with books, with a bong resting on top like Excalibur erupting from the stone. They were ancient paperbacks, the covers tattered and worn, edges frayed and torn. The image on each cover was a freeze-frame depiction of crime, and they all had titles like *The Sour Lemon Score* and *The Name of the Game is Death* and *Hell Hath No Fury*.

"Jesus, who thought up these titles?" she said as she tossed each one onto the tabletop.

A small cafe-style table rested outside the bathroom door. Two guitars were propped up on stands. One was acoustic and the other electric, and both looked to have cost a decent bit of cash. Whatever money Billy had, this was where it went.

Papers were scattered across the table. Crash pushed them around with the end of a pen. Sheet music. Guitar parts for various songs. Some Eagles, some Skynyrd. From Billy working to learn songs for The Nightside Regulars. He seemed like the type who would throw himself completely into something, no matter how useless or futile it seemed.

Crash shifted the papers around. Bills and credit card offers and wildlife groups wanting money and printouts from newspapers.

Crash looked at the printouts. A newspaper article, from the county paper's website. The headline read: "Daring Bank Holdup Nets Half-Million Dollar Haul."

Her eyes scanned across the words, anticipating what was coming, but she knew already.

The Guthrie National Bank robbery.

She found other printouts about the second robbery. About

the bank teller killed.

Then she found the articles about Gary Campbell and Campbell's Market, and her heart sank.

Chapter 23

Matt met Crash at Billy's apartment. A woman watched through the living room curtains as he pulled into the driveway and parked behind Crash's cruiser. She kept her eyes on Matt as he ascended the stairs into the garage apartment. He was winded once he reached the top, and he leaned into the doorframe and caught his breath.

Crash was at the cafe table, assembling papers into stacks. She said, "You okay?"

"The lady of the house gave me the hairy eyeball the whole time I was coming up here."

"I think she's nervous thinking we'll bust her for letting the son of pot farmers live here."

"Can you arrest someone for that?"

"Almost positive you can't unless she's contributing to a crime. Which I'm sure she isn't."

Matt walked into the apartment, surveying the space. "Might be fun to mess with her."

"Almost any other day I'd be all in for that, but there're larger issues at play here."

Matt put on gloves and walked over to the table. Crash had put everything into neat, orderly stacks. She pointed to one stack. The top sheet was a newspaper printout.

"That's the stuff on the two bank holdups," she said. She gestured to another stack. "That's what they put together on

Campbell and Carlton."

Matt flipped through the papers. Billy had put together a history of the business lives of Gary Campbell and Peter Carlton.

"Campbell closed up shop three months after the bank robberies," Matt said. "Carlton made a stronger go of it a little while longer, but he still folded within a year."

"Someone saw a connection between Campbell and Carlton and the bank robberies."

"Why, though? And why the attacks?"

"Because if Campbell and Carlton had something to do with those bank robberies then somehow they can get money from it now."

"Those robberies, that's more than fifteen years ago. That money's long gone by now."

"You've got two old guys who still have names, respect in the community. Reputations to uphold. That's bound to be worth something."

"Blackmail?"

Crash shrugged. "I'm spitballing ideas here. Any idea is better than nothing."

"A world full of bad ideas out there would argue that point with you." She held up a finger. "Oh, and I can't forget this."

Crash disappeared into another room and came back holding a security guard uniform on a hanger. She showed Matt the patch sewn onto the arm. Tri-Comm.

"Seems Billy was moonlighting," Matt said.

"It's the kind of job that would give him access to security codes," Crash said. "So he could get into the Campbell house."

There was a soft knocking at the apartment door, and Matt and Crash turned to see the wife standing in the doorway, her hands twisted together. She shifted back and forth like she needed to pee and the line for the bathroom was too long.

Matt walked toward the door. "Hello, ma'am."

"Listen, I hate to ask this and all, but I'm wondering how long you all are going to be here, on account I've now got two police cars sitting in my driveway, and my neighbors—"

"You have neighbors?" Crash said. The tone was more astonished than anything.

The woman's face dropped. "Yes, Deputy, I've got neighbors. Not many, because who wants a house like this in a place like this, but the neighbors I've got, they're calling me, asking what's going on."

"And what are you telling them?" Matt said.

"What the hell do you think I'm telling them? I'm telling them my dumbass husband let the guy he's buying pot from live in our garage." She buried her face in her hands and shook her head. "My dad told me I could have done better. Why didn't I listen to him?"

Matt and Crash parked in the lot outside the cookie factory and waited. They sat in silence, waiting for the shift whistle to blow, eyes trained on the exit gate.

The whistle shrieked, and five minutes later, Gloria Miller came through the gate and headed toward a beat-to-hell minivan. Her shoulders were slumped, her face drawn, her movements implying each step was a struggle.

"Come on," Crash said and reached to open her door, and realized Matt didn't respond. His head was slumped against the driver's side window, his eyes closed, a gentle snoring sound rolling out of him.

She patted his arm. He stirred awake, eyes popping open like pulled blinds, his expression startled and shocked. He wiped at the corners of his mouth, pushing away imagined drool. His eyes flitted for a moment, and he looked embarrassed.

"Sorry about that," he said. "I'm tired."

Crash smiled. "Guess so." She pointed out the window. "Gloria's coming."

Gloria's face glowed with hopefulness as Matt and Crash approached from across the parking lot. She set her purse and lunch bag on the ground next to her minivan and threw herself around Matt.

"Did you find her?" she said, her head pressed into his chest.

Matt took her shoulders and pried himself loose of her. The light glistening in her eyes goddamn near broke Matt's heart.

"Not yet, but there are leads," he said. "There's a few questions we need to ask you, and they might not be questions you like."

Gloria's face turned hard and confused. "What the hell are you saying, Matt?" She spun her attention over to Crash. "What's going on with my girl?"

Crash said, "Why don't we sit in the van and talk."

Which they did. Gloria in the driver's seat, Matt and Crash behind her. The van was cluttered with fast food wrappers and clots of dirt and Lego pieces and french fries that would never, ever go away.

Gloria twisted herself to face Matt and Crash. A tidal wave of conflicting emotions washed over her face. Frustration, anticipation, fear.

Matt said, "Do you know Gary Campbell? Or Peter Carlton?"

Her expression flipped to confusion. "You're not making sense, Matt. What do they have to do—"

"Just answer the question, Gloria. Please. What about Gary Campbell or Peter Carlton?"

Gloria sighed. "Gary Campbell. Yeah, I know him. I mean, I haven't seen him in—Jesus Christ—well, back before Micki. Tyson worked at one of Mr. Campbell's stores."

Crash said, "What did your husband do for Campbell?"

"He clerked at the Campbell's Market off of 232. Stocked shelves, mopped up when someone's stupid kid shattered a bottle of ketchup or a jar of pickles on the floor. Tyson hated it, but after I got pregnant, he said he wanted to do something different with himself. Said it was important that he be this new person since he was going to be a father." She smiled. "Before he disappeared, he started reading all the time. Always had a little book in his hand. Wanted to be smart enough to be a better dad than what he had."

"When did you talk to Campbell last?" Matt said.

"It's a small town, Matt. I'm sure I've said hi to him here and there a million times. But if you mean an actual conversation past two people being polite, it's not been since Tyson vanished off to wherever it was he went. Mr. Campbell came by himself to drop off Tyson's last paycheck, and he gave us extra bags of groceries. Said on account of Tyson leaving, that he was disappointed with him disappearing the way he did. Mr. Campbell had been working with him, coming by the house. Tyson said Mr. Campbell was getting him ready for management." Gloria laughed. "I never pictured Tyson running a store, anything like that, but they'd sit in the dining room and talk for hours, sounding very serious."

Crash and Matt exchanged looks. Crash said, "Do you know what they were talking about?"

"No idea. I was pregnant with Micki, and they'd all be in there smoking and drinking coffee, and I couldn't be around all of that, so I kept to myself in the living room. I was learning to knit and trying to make Micki a blanket, so I—"

"Did anyone else come with Campbell during these visits?"

"A few times, a guy came by. I don't remember his name. All of this is ancient history, Matt." She sniffed. "I want my daughter back. She's all I've got left of Tyson. The boys are wonderful, but their dad was never any account, and I'd just as soon forget him and be thankful for what he gave me. Tyson, though, that was the one real love I got out of my life, no matter what sort of asshole he was, and Micki's the only piece of that." She looked at them both with sad eyes, as if trying to hide a secret shame. "You might think I'm a pathetic old woman for still loving someone like Tyson, but that's the way it is sometimes. You can't help who you love."

Matt rested his hand on hers. "We're doing everything we can to bring her home to you, Gloria." He squeezed her hand gently. "About the other man who met with Tyson and Campbell. Are you sure you don't remember his name?"

"I don't. I'm sorry. All this, it's nothing I've given two breaths thinking about for years now. Is any of this going to help you find Micki?"

"It might. I wouldn't be asking if I didn't think it would."

"I don't get what Gary Campbell and Tyson have to do with Micki being missing, though."

"It's complicated, so I need you to let us work this, and don't talk about it with anyone, please. Trust us on this. Can you do that?"

"If it's for Micki."

Matt slid open the side door so he and Crash could get out. Gloria rolled down her window.

"You'll tell me when you find something, right?" she said.

"We'll call as soon as we find out anything," Matt said. "One last thing. Where were you and Tyson living when all of this was going on?"

"There was a trailer park out on Route 68, and we rented this shitty little single-wide. It was a fucking dump. The roof leaked, the floors were falling in, and anytime the wind blew, you'd think for sure the damn thing would topple over or cave in. But we were kids and didn't know any better and didn't have nowhere else to go, anyway. After Tyson left, I couldn't even afford the rent on it, so I had to move to Section 8 housing. Jesus but that was even worse."

Matt nodded. "Thanks for talking. Thanks for trusting us."

"I wouldn't if it were almost anyone else. But why d'you ask about that old trailer?"

"No reason, Gloria. Just curious, that's all."

Gloria's minivan turned out of the lot and faded into the distance down the road. Matt folded his arms across the roof of the cruiser and rested his head there.

"Goddammit," he said.

"What do you want to do, Sheriff?" Crash said.

Matt lifted his head and looked at Crash. "Calling me Sheriff again. Never a good sign."

"This situation is what the classicists would refer to as a 'giant clusterfuck,' and I may be out of my element, so I'm opting to lean on your many years of experience."

"That feels distinctly like a dig at my age."

"Look at it instead as me saying you've done this for only slightly fewer years than I've been breathing, so you may have a better idea of what to do next."

"That definitely feels like you're calling me old." Matt opened his door. "Let's go talk to Gary Campbell."

"He hasn't been too interested in talking to us before now."

"Shit changes. He's going to have to find himself interested."

Chapter 24

Matt and Crash found the business card Matt had left stuck in the front door was still there.

From the car, Matt called the hospital. He talked to someone for a few moments, hung up, and said, "Campbell's not there, either."

"Drive me back to the courthouse. I'll get my truck and stake out this place. I can take a spot down the street, and he won't notice my truck the way if I was in a county cruiser. You want to take the hospital?"

"Sure. Might be the same spot Campbell's daughter parked at when she told herself she caught her father cheating on her mother."

"You suppose there's any irony in that?"

"Nope. Irony died in all of this fuck-up a while back." Matt took a deep breath. "I'm not sure I can keep this shit up much longer, Crash."

"I don't blame you. You're old as fuck."

"You can stop that shit anytime you want. Me getting older isn't the worry. Honestly, it beats all the other options. I'm just tired of people being assholes to each other."

"You're tough, Matt. You've got this."

"Yeah. Sure I do."

Matt sat in the hospital parking lot, his cruiser pointed toward the entrance. He had driven by the Riverside and picked up a roast beef sandwich and fries and coffee. He ate most of the sandwich, but the fries were cold and soggy. All the meals from the Riverside he'd consumed from Styrofoam takeout containers, he kept a higher level of expectation for the food he'd eat if he sat down there. He sipped at his coffee. At least he had that.

He called Rachel and let her know he wouldn't be home for a while. She wasn't happy, but she accepted it, the way she had always accepted his long hours at work. Their first time around, shit like this had happened more nights than it didn't.

Now, her tone was different. Now was a begrudging acceptance of situation and circumstances. She knew this couldn't last forever. There was the elephant in the room he didn't want to discuss. The Big C. Rachel, she was good to talk about it. She wanted to understand it, to help her understand Matt.

Hadn't been that way when he told her. Not at first. No, in those initial weeks, she dug her heels in and acted like it was nothing. Like it was a cold or the goddamn flu. She had seemed determined to pretend it all away. That didn't work, though, because it wasn't an answer that ever worked.

So she changed tactics. She studied up on liver cancer. There were books about it all around the house and websites bookmarked on the computer. She pushed him to go to a support group. He refused, so she went instead when she found one for partners of cancer patients and survivors.

And she made plans. God love her, she made these big plans for when he left office. At first, she wanted him to resign, or take medical leave, but they both understood that would never happen. He told her he didn't know the meaning of the word *quit*. She offered to buy him a dictionary. He agreed not to run for another term, and they would make life plans for what happened after that.

Matt hoped to discover what would happen after that.

The sun set low in the distance, and the sky darkened, with

gray clouds threatening overhead. He could almost smell the rain brewing.

His phone rang. It was Amy, Carl's sister. Crying.

"Amy?" he said.

More sobbing. "Matt? Matt?" Her voice was rushed and exhausted at the same time.

Matt bolted up in his seat. "Amy? What's wrong?"

"It's Carl. He's locked in his room." Something crashed and shattered in the background. "He's got a gun, Matt." A breath. "He's got his gun."

The line went quiet. In the background, Matt heard a faraway voice. A man's voice. Angry.

Matt strapped his seat belt on and started the engine. "I'm on my way."

Amy's face was red and blotchy as she ran to Matt in the driveway. She had to bend at the waist to rest her head on Matt's shoulder as she slung her arms around him and cried.

"What happened?" Matt said.

She pulled back and wiped away tears. "I was in the kitchen, making dinner. Michael's coming home from Clarksburg with the girls. Carl was in the bathroom, and then he was screaming and cursing. He slammed his bedroom door shut and the lock snapped shut. I banged on the door and asked what happened, and then I smelled something coming from the bathroom—"

Matt nodded.

"I heard him getting into his gun box. I told him to let me in, and he said to leave him alone, that he had a gun. He said it like it was a warning."

"And you're sure about the pistol? He's not bullshitting you?"

"Yes. It's a .45 our dad owned."

"Okay. I need you to call Tim and tell him to meet you by Dairy Queen, and get the girls ice cream. Don't tell him anything because you don't want him to have to play a scenario out in front of everyone. Stay out there for a while and I'll call you, give you the all-clear."

"Are you going to call anyone? Call the police?"

Matt smiled. "I am the police. But I'm also Carl's friend, and that's the more important thing right now. Calling me was the right decision. Now I need you to get the hell out of here." He rested his hand on her warm, wet cheek. "He's a stubborn son of a bitch. Always has been."

Chapter 25

Matt pressed his ear against the door to Carl's bedroom. Bob Dylan played. "All Along the Watchtower."

The smell from the bathroom down the hall still hung heavy. The stench of piss and shit. Droplets of something dark on the hardwood floor led out of the bathroom and into Carl's bedroom.

Matt took a deep breath through his mouth and knocked on the door.

Inside the room, Carl said, "Goddammit, Amy, I—"

"It's Matt, Carl."

The pause lasted a while. Carl said, "Get the fuck out of here now, Matt. This ain't got shit to do with you."

"Brother, you and I both know that's not happening, so you may as well roll your ass over here and open this goddamn door."

"Fuck off, Matt. I'm not in the mood."

"And you think I am? Your sister's scared shitless. It's not like I don't have fifty other things I could be doing, so you are aware."

"I didn't ask you to come here, Matt."

"No, you did not. Your sister did, because you're acting like a horse's ass. Now I'll ask you one more time to open this door. If you don't, I'll kick it in."

Carl laughed—almost more of a snort—but there was movement in the room, and the lock on the door clicked. Matt opened the door as Carl wheeled himself back toward the center of the room.

The stink in the bedroom was worse than what had been in the hallway. Something soaked Carl's sweatpants as though he'd spilled coffee all over his lap. The .45 rested on his thigh, away from the stain.

Carl's bedroom was decorated as an altar to his former life, though it felt more like a memorial for someone who had died. Framed newspaper clippings from his high school and college football days were mounted on the wall. Carl had played defense and tackle at Marshall, and football trophies lined a shelf. Citations for bravery and commendations for excellence in duty hung next to pictures of Carl and Matt on fishing trips. In one, they stood next to one another, each holding their catch. Carl towered over Matt, but Matt's fish was a beast compared to the minnow Carl held in his oversized hands.

The pictures seemed like ancient history, though Matt remembered vividly. Two or three years ago at most for them. Hell, they seemed like yesterday sometimes. They hurt to look at or to think about.

"Where's Amy?" Carl faced the window. The wind stirred outside, and branches from the oak trees on the side of the house whipped against the glass.

"She's headed down the road."

"You tell her to leave?"

"I did."

Carl's hand patted the .45. "What you expecting on happening here, Matt?"

Matt stepped toward Carl. "Depends."

Carl's hand wrapped around the .45. His finger slid against the trigger as his hand folded around the grip. Carl's focus stayed locked on the window. "On?"

Matt froze, his eyes focused on the gun. "Depends on what you're planning on doing."

Carl sighed. "I'd like to go on vacation. Somewhere they've

got dark-skinned, big-titted women who'll serve you drinks from hollowed-out tropical fruit, and they'll call you 'American Joe' and they don't mind that your dick doesn't work."

"I'm pretty sure what you want to do is be in one of those movies about Vietnam vets, because none of that shit has happened in thirty years, I'm almost positive."

"Easy for you to say; your dick works."

Matt made a step toward Carl. Carl twitched ever so slightly, but he didn't respond otherwise. He kept a firm hold on his pistol.

"Stay where you're at, Matt." Carl's voice was cold and flat.

Matt reached his right hand out, palm up. "Why don't you give me that gun?"

Carl remained still. "Why'd you tell Amy to leave?"

"Thought it might be better if she wasn't around for this."

Carl rolled closer to the window. "*For this*? What's this, Matt? Is it where I shove this gun against the roof of my mouth and pull the trigger? Because you and I both know, you do shit like that, you've got to be sure you're blowing out a substantial amount of brain matter. Clean out the really important parts. Not like that guy a few years back? You remember him? The high school janitor."

"I remember. He had come back from a deployment in Afghanistan. PTSD."

"That's right. Fuck. I'd forgotten that. The wife, she left him, didn't she? Took the kids with her?"

"She did."

Carl said, "Yeah, what I remember is that all he did was shove the gun to the back of his throat and *boom*. What that did was take out the back half of his skull. He realized what had happened, and he had to call 911 himself. Once he got out of the hospital and went into rehab, he hung himself with a bedsheet." Carl lifted the gun and gestured it for emphasis. "That type of determination, that's what really makes this nation incredible. We'll keep doing something stupid until we get it right. But that is not how I want to go out. I'm scoring for more of a one-and-done situation. No need to hang around and linger, because then what's the point, right?"

"Carl—"

Carl spun around, and he aimed the gun at Matt. "What about a murder-suicide? What do you think of that? You've got cancer, I'm in this chair. Everyone will think we opted to take this way out to end the suffering."

Matt didn't flinch. Didn't even move. Kept his eyes trained on Carl. "Can we leave behind a note for everyone first? Something that goes on about how no one would understand our 'love that dare not speak its name'?"

Carl sighed. "Goddammit. Just goddammit all." His arm dropped and swung next to his chair, the gun pointed toward the ground. His head fell forward, shoulders slouched, and it was almost as though he were praying.

Matt considered moving again. He could get closer and grab the gun from Carl. But even in the wheelchair, Carl was a big man, and he could knock Matt across the room with little effort.

Instead, he crouched onto his haunches and leaned backward until he balanced on his heels and his shoulder blades hit the wall.

"You want to do this?" Matt said.

Carl lifted his head. He wouldn't look at Matt. "Do what?"

"Jesus fuck, Carl, play Monopoly. You reek of piss and you've got a goddamn gun, so it feels like the options here are few. Kill yourself. That. That what you want?"

"I think so. I don't know. Some days are better. Days like that, I'm okay with this. I'm not good with it, but it's what it is. Other days—" The words drifted off and faded into nothing.

"Days like today."

"Yeah."

"What happened?"

"I had to empty the bag. Amy usually helps, but you can't keep asking your sister to dump your piss into the toilet, so I tried it myself. I was in the bathroom, and I had it unhooked and I was dumping it in the toilet, and this boom of thunder came from nowhere, and I twitched when it did, so—"

Matt waited for the next words, but they didn't come from Carl. Instead, Carl stared off into the distance.

"Can I have the gun?" Matt said.

Carl shook his head again. "No."

"You're not doing this, Carl. Give me the gun, let's get you cleaned up, and then—"

"I want back out there. This isn't what I signed up for. Do you not get this is all I am now? Some useless pile of shit in a wheelchair?" He lifted his arm and raised the gun in the air.

Matt came to his feet. Carl swung his arm around and aimed the pistol at Matt.

Matt's hands went up, and he stared at the barrel of the gun. A small smile curled up from his lips, and he laughed. His hands dropped. Carl kept a steady aim at him.

"Go ahead," Matt said. He took another step forward. "Pull the trigger. Do it."

"I don't want to, but I will. You can just turn around and leave, Matt."

"That's not happening. Your options are hand me the weapon or you shoot me. And I need to be super clear here about one thing: I don't give a fuck if you shoot me, so this, it's not even a threat." Another step forward. "I'm already dying, you stupid, selfish son of a bitch. Christ, but you're a fucking asshole, Carl, and you don't even realize it."

Carl's hand trembled, but he kept the gun aimed at Matt's chest.

Another step from Matt. Maybe two feet between him and the gun. He could have snatched the gun from Carl's hand.

"You sit here and whine about being in a goddamn wheelchair, whereas in six months, I'm most likely going to be in a coffin. Your ignorant ass wants me to knock up my wife so she can have a kid I'll never see, and you're fine. No, you can't walk. No, you're in this goddamn chair. You know what? I'd give anything to be in that goddamn chair. I'm sick and tired of cancer. I'm sick and tired of waking up every day, kind of surprised that I'm waking up, and going through every day knowing I'm dying. And not dying in that 'Hey, we're all dying a day at a time' bullshit. I'm dying in the 'Fuck, I might not make it to see the next *Star Wars* movie' way. I'm dying in the way that doesn't get to be stoic and dignified. That's my life, Carl, so pardon me if I don't feel sorry for you because you had an oopsie moment and you got shit on you, because at this moment, my insides are literally being eaten away by my own body."

Matt reached out and grabbed the pistol. He didn't pull it away but instead raised it higher, leveling it even with his chest. Carl watched Matt with an escalating look of surprise. Matt let go of his hold on the gun's barrel.

"So there you go," he said. "You wanna do this shit, do it now, and let's move on with our deaths. Otherwise, let go of that goddamn gun before I take it and beat the ever-loving fuck out of you with it."

Carl stared at Matt for what seemed forever. Matt would have sworn he heard a clock ticking away somewhere in the house.

Carl flipped the gun around, clutched the barrel, and handed it to Matt. Matt took the pistol by the grip. He racked the round out of the chamber and popped out the clip.

Carl bowed his head like a kid ashamed of his behavior. Matt walked over to him, steadied himself behind Carl's wheelchair, and pushed him toward the door.

"You need to lose weight, Carl," Matt said. "You're getting fat."

"Fuck you, Matt." There was laughter in the words.

Chapter 26

"You see anything?" Matt said.

"No," Crash said. "Didn't see anything three minutes ago when you asked me the same goddamn question."

Matt let out a low whistle. They sat in the cab of Crash's pickup, staring at the driveway to Gary Campbell's house. Where they had been sitting for hours. Matt parked his car—he had driven home and traded out his cruiser for his Ford Focus—behind the pickup and joined Crash inside the truck two hours earlier. Crash had already been there a few hours. It reflected in her attitude.

"Grumpy?" Matt said.

"Tired. And I need to pee."

"So go pee."

"Where? We're not out in the middle of the woods, and lest you forget—and I suspect that you do—I can't just whip it out and let it go the way you can."

"I forget sometimes that—"

"I'm female?"

"Yeah."

"How's that happen?"

"Enough time in uniform, being a cop identifies you more than if you're a guy or a woman. The army's the same way. You stop seeing male or female and all you're left with is the uniform."

"Must have made dating difficult."

"You learn early on not to shit where you sleep."

"Good rule in life."

Crash shifted in her seat. She was small, with her deep green eyes and freckles that splattered across her nose. Never any makeup. When she became a deputy, the department had to special order her uniforms since they had nothing close to anything that would have fit her.

But then he remembered the times he watched her take down men twice her size. Drunks whenever they had to clear out a bar, or angry husbands during domestic calls, or hostile drivers unhappy they had gotten pulled over for speeding, shocked this little thing wasn't blown away by their charm and rushing to tear up their speeding ticket. The cute little deputy who was a black belt in Brazilian jiujitsu could flip an asshole over her shoulder and have zip cuffs on them before they had a second to know what happened.

Once it was understood Carl wasn't coming back, it hadn't been a reluctance by the other deputies knowing that Crash would step into the man's large shoes. The friendship between Matt and Carl outside the office was known, and they watched Matt struggle in the wake of the shooting. No, the truth was, despite being young and small and seemingly nothing more but a hiring intended to fill a quota, Crash was the best person for the job.

The thought crossed his mind sometimes. She's young enough. She could be like his daughter.

"That's him right there."

Crash's voice.

Matt watched as the car passed them and turned up Campbell's driveway. "Give him a minute, and then we'll go up."

Crash started the truck's engine. "Fuck that. We're talking to him now." She shifted the truck into first and pulled out. "Besides, I still need to pee."

The lights were on inside the house as Crash parked her truck behind Campbell's car.

They took the steps up onto the front porch. Matt pushed the doorbell. Two seconds later, he pounded on the front door.

Crash leaned into the door. "I hear him in there."

"Not surprising since we saw him walk in." Matt slammed the side of his fist on the door again. "Campbell! It's the sheriff's department! We know you're in there! Open this door up now! We need to talk!"

The front door jerked open and Campbell, his face flushed beneath the fading bruises and the bandages, stared at Matt and Crash through the screen door.

"What the hell is your goddamn problem?" he said. His voice was harsh, his breathing short. "You've got no right to—"

"Where's Tyson Miller?" Matt said.

Campbell's eyebrows shifted backward a little. His face relaxed a fraction, only to change to an expression of panic. A move from offense to defense.

"What are you talking about?" Campbell said.

"Tyson Miller," Crash said. "He worked for one of your stores about fifteen years ago and then he vanished."

Campbell's laugh. Mocking and derisive. "Are you serious? You expect me to remember everyone who ever worked for me? Christ, I ran that business for thirty years. I wasn't out there hiring in the individual stores. The managers hired stock clerks."

"Who said he was a stock clerk?" Matt said.

"I'm assuming—"

"Don't assume. Assuming anything right now isn't your friend. You mind letting us in so we can talk?"

"I do mind. I'm here to pick up a few things and get back to the hospital."

Crash stepped toward Campbell. In that action, she seemed a giant. Campbell drew back as if Crash had raised a fist to him. What force of will could do for a person was a remarkable thing.

"Was Miller involved when you and Carlton robbed the Guthrie National Bank?" she said.

Matt groaned. Obviously they were abandoning tact and the element of surprise.

Crash had that gift for putting everything right there on the table, laying it all out for the world to see. She was a blunt object, a baseball bat through a windshield, a crowbar to the back of the knees. Effective, yes, but she didn't leave anyone much play with subtlety.

Campbell said, "If both of you aren't off of my front porch in one minute and out of my driveway in two, I'll be on the phone with the state police and have real cops—"

"Why did you lie to us about the night of the attack?" Matt said.

Campbell paused. Sucked in some air. He gestured at Matt with a raised finger ready to speak, but the words caught somewhere in his throat and he stood there, letting them roll around without releasing them.

Matt said, "The security footage only shows two people entering and exiting your house. They look nothing like what you described to us. There's a reason you lied to us, and we need you to tell us the truth."

Campbell shook his head. "Have you lost your mind, Sheriff? This cancer I've heard you've got, it's affected your brain. I was in shock that night. Beaten half to death. I have doctors telling me my wife's going to die, that I have to decide to pull the plug on her life support. And you have the balls to stand there and accuse me of lying to you?"

Matt nodded. "I do, because you did lie to us. I think you and Carlton and Tyson Miller robbed the Guthrie National Bank, and that's why you were both attacked, and the way things are going, it will end with the two of you. There's either other people involved, or the people who attacked you, they'll keep on pushing you for what it is they want. Which leaves you with two choices: give up and give in to them, or push back. You might not do the former, but I'll bet you're willing to try the latter, and you'll ignore they're young and brutal and you are an old man waiting out the days he's got left. Or you can take what's behind door number three, which is to tell us what happened and let us figure out a way to stop them before anyone else gets hurt."

Campbell stared at them. Matt could see all the years lived on the old man's face, and others accumulated in the past week. Matt wondered about what it meant to be old. To know your days were numbered, and to have to accept that you had fewer ahead of you than you had behind you. He supposed that, looking at life that way, he knew what it meant to be old.

Campbell said, "Come on inside."

Chapter 27

Campbell offered to make a pot of coffee as Matt and Crash took seats at the kitchen table. Matt declined; accepting hospitality felt like giving in, however minuscule that might seem, and he wanted to keep as much control of the situation as possible.

Campbell moved in degrees and inches, bit by bit, and he winced in pain as he made his way to his chair. He sat down in a slow, creeping movement, like a car being lowered on a lift. Once his ass hit the seat, he let out a long breath of air as if he were being depressurized. Whatever fight the old man had possessed—the fight that had kept him in business, had made him lie to Matt and Crash, had made him keep trying to win at a game no one else was playing—all left his body. What remained was a bruised and battered shell of a proud man.

Matt said, "Did you rob the Guthrie National Bank?"

Campbell said, "Yes. Myself, Peter Carlton, Frank Dodson, Roger Waits, and Tyson Miller."

"Who's Roger Waits?" Crash said.

"The secretary for the Benevolent Order of the Everlasting Knights."

"The group from the picture in the living room?" Matt said.

Campbell nodded. "Peter, Roger, Frank, and myself, we all belonged. Not Miller, though. The Order, they'd have never let in someone like him. The rest of us, we were all businessmen. Peter owned the construction company, I owned the stores, Frank had the corner of the floral market for the county, and Roger did the books for most of the businesses in Serenity. Miller wasn't what the Order was looking for."

"Because he had been a criminal."

"If you're looking to be blunt about it, then yes."

"You haven't seen *blunt* yet. Was it you four who came to him to rob the banks?"

"We did. The world was changing. We were all struggling. The chains moved in and they stayed open all night, with grocery stores and clothing and they'd change the oil in your car and sell you tires, all under one roof. One of those big box stores was larger than three of my markets combined, and they undercut my prices. It hit us all there toward the end of the Nineties, as the coal mines were either laying people off or closing operations down whole. Machines could pull the coal it used to take ten or twenty men to pull, so they needed fewer people. Everyone had less money, so they shopped somewhere else. My stores had been there since my father opened the first one back in 1952, and we made sure to know everyone who came through the door. None of that mattered when people just had fewer dollars to spend. You can't begrudge anyone for doing the best thing for their families."

"Then try telling us how robbing a bank would fix your problem," Crash said. Her words cut in a bitter and brash tone.

Bad cop, Matt thought.

"You don't understand, Deputy," Campbell said. "I wanted to fight it. I planned to renovate the stores, expand them and shine them up, and I thought maybe that would encourage people to come back to what they knew. I added delis and a floral department. I looked around and tried to see what people wanted."

"You couldn't renovate enough to change what had already been changed, though," Matt said.

The old man's body slumped in a sense of remembered defeat. "I found that out late down the road. At first, I dug into my pockets and spent what I had. Then I went to the banks, but

THE RIGHTEOUS PATH

they turned me down. Said it wasn't a good risk. Decades in business meant nothing. The remodels were half-finished, and there was no money to finish things. Roger told me he knew investors out of Clarksburg who might help me. I sat down with them and we talked. Roger left out the part about the investors being with the mob."

Crash ran her hands through her hair. "Are you telling us you borrowed money from the mafia? Where has that ever been a good idea?"

Campbell raised his chin in the air. Tried to look proud and defiant. "Tomorrow, go out and talk to people about those stores. Ask around. I'll bet at one time or another you had a family member without food in their house—maybe they'd lost their job, or the dad drank his paycheck, or whatever the reason—and they talked to me and left with the groceries to feed their children that night. When they could, they gave it back. Not always, but almost always. If the marching band needed new uniforms, I bought them. Plenty of my profits paid for school trips and events for children who wouldn't have gone otherwise. Go to a big box store today and see what happens. I won't pretend what I did was a good idea, but I refused to let all of that fade away into nothing, and I won't apologize for it."

Matt cleared his throat. "Enough. What happened after you spoke to the mob guys?"

Campbell shrugged. "We talked and I got the money, finished the work on the stores, and then nothing. There was a little spark for a few months. Classic false hope, I guess. I hired new people. Put up new signs. Ads on TV and radio. But the tide, it'd already turned, and the next quarter, things were worse, and I was even deeper in debt. I was neck deep in with men who wanted their money back, and I had nothing to give them. Pete didn't borrow money, but he struggled also because no money coming into the county meant no one built anything. Hell, his company did the store renovations, and I owed him for that work. Businesses closed and left Roger without books to balance. Frank realized no one buys bouquets of roses when the rest of the world is falling apart. There we all were, sitting with what everyone said was the American dream, and we were all choking to death on it."

"Who came up with the idea of the bank robbery?"

"Roger. He said Guthrie National received a large deposit every Monday morning after the businesses from the mall dumped everything in the night deposit over the weekend. They processed the deposits, and an armored truck came by right at ten in the morning. He said with the four of us, plus another guy, we could swoop in, grab the money before the truck got there, and vanish."

Matt caught himself staring at Campbell. He hoped his mouth wasn't open, with the look people get when someone's telling them an idea that seems so stupid, you wonder how it had been allowed to even form, how it got there, how the person sitting in front of you had gotten this far in life without somehow jabbing a fork in their eye or falling down an open manhole, if they believed what they had described was a good idea.

Crash interrupted Matt's thoughts by saying, "Waits thought this up?"

"He did," Campbell said.

"And you and the others tagged along with it?"

"No one else had any other ideas. The men in Clarksburg wouldn't take no for an answer when they came looking for their money."

"Was this guy Waits nothing but a bad idea factory?"

Campbell lowered his head. "We found out later he had a huge coke problem. He owed twenty grand to a dealer out of Pittsburgh, and the dealer wanted his money back also."

"Where's Waits at now?" Matt said.

"Dead. Massive heart attack a year after everything happened. Idiot wouldn't stop shoving everything up his nose, and it caught up with him."

"Okay, so you morons decided you wanted to rob banks," Crash said. "How'd Tyson Miller get involved?"

"Miller worked at the store here in Serenity. Everyone knows the Millers; they're not worth the paper it'd take to wipe their asses, but Tyson, he said he wanted to end that cycle and wanted to clean up his life. He had a kid coming, he told Rich Watson—he was the store manager back then—that he needed something regular and steady, and with his reputation most places wouldn't take the chance on him, but Rich said he seemed so sincere."

Crash blew air out of her nose. "This guy looking for a second chance, and you saw a stooge."

"I saw a guy without much to lose. He worked at the store, but how long do you suppose it would have lasted? Guys like Miller don't stick to anything respectable for long."

"I'd watch throwing aspersions around people when you're in the middle of admitting to bank robberies."

Campbell shrugged. "We hired certain types to stock shelves and bag groceries. High school kids, retirees, the occasional retard, but most of what we got were ones who get hired anywhere else. We knew we needed someone with some criminal experience, so I flipped through the employment files and found Tyson, and I caught him as he came out of the store at the end of a shift, asked him to meet us all at a bar over in Madison, in Guthrie County. Roger, Pete, Tyson, Frank, and me. We told him what the plan was. He hedged off at first. He was nervous about the whole thing. All he'd done prior was penny ante things like shoplifting, breaking into cars—small-time things. Robbing a bank is federal prison time. He wasn't sure about it."

"What about you?" Crash said. "Your family? Your business? None of that crossed your mind?"

"They were all I thought about, Deputy. Which was why I chose to go through with it. My family would have nothing if I didn't. We all knew we were in the same boat and that we didn't have another choice."

"Except Miller," Matt said. "Miller could have walked away

and been fine."

"Was your job being devil's advocate?" Crash said. "Tell him what he'd be able to give the kid he had coming? All the stuff a guy like him never imagined his kid having?"

Campbell looked down at his hands. He kept on talking.

"We decided on a day to do it. We met multiple times to plan things out. Usually at Miller's house. It'd be Roger driving, with Pete, Tyson, Frank, and myself in the bank. Tyson stole a car for us to use, and he got us the guns. We figured out the layout of the bank and the quickest ways in and out. Then—" He took a deep breath. "We did it."

"And got away with it," Matt said.

"We did. None of us understood how. Like how you see it in the movies. No one gave us any problems. Smooth and clean and neat."

"You came out on the other end seven hundred grand richer."

"Enough to pay back what I owed, with some left to split."

"Why do it again, then? Why take the risk twice?"

"Because we were greedy and stupid and cocky. Because the police and the Feds and everyone else, they kept looking for us, and nothing tied us to the robbery. No one saw our faces. No one ID'd our voices. It seemed so simple and easy—"

"You thought you could do it all over again."

"We did. We all thought, 'Why not make a little more money?' Just some extra, with a bigger share for everyone this time. No one would expect us to hit it again two weeks later."

"The bank teller," Crash said. "Why kill her?"

"No one was ever supposed to die, Deputy. We weren't killers. We weren't criminals. Except for Miller, but even he wasn't a murderer." A beat. "Roger. He kept doing more coke. It was constant, always excusing himself to go to the bathroom and coming back with his eyes wild, and he had all of this twitchy, nervous energy. The morning of the second robbery, he changed the plan at the last minute and said he wanted to come into the bank this time and Miller to drive. Roger wanted to be a part of the action himself. But he was different that morning. Shaky and agitated, on edge about everything."

"Did anyone stop and say letting a coked-up asshole help rob a bank seemed like a bad idea?" Crash said.

"We were too far in. We were greedy and stupid. It had gone off without a hitch the first time, so we kept telling ourselves we could do it again."

"Was it Roger who shot the teller?" Matt said.

"Yes. She was slipping the dye pack in one of the bags, and he happened to see her. He didn't even take a breath when he did it. He yelled something at her, then he fired, and—"

Matt held his hands in the air. "That's enough. Tell us about after the robbery. We can account for you, Carlton, Dodson, and Waits, but Miller vanished. And you know what happened to him, don't you?"

Campbell's head dropped. "I don't know, Sheriff." His hands grasped his bald head. "I don't know."

"Bullshit," Crash said. The word came out as an angry hiss, and she slammed her fist on the table. Campbell jolted upright and drew backward, his face pale, as if he was ready to have a heart attack. "There's no way you don't know where he is. You pricks killed him so that there'd be one less person to split the cash with."

Matt set his hand on Crash's shoulder and pulled her back into her chair. Her eyes shifted over to him. She was a clenched fist, angry and wanting to strike out. Matt squeezed her shoulder slightly, and she took a deep breath and settled back into the chair.

Matt walked around the table to be closer to Campbell. "Campbell, you're an old man already staring at federal prison time, so you are running out of things to lose. Lying to us will not help your situation. Tell us what happened to Miller. Let a woman know what happened to her husband. Give her that much mercy."

Campbell turned away from Matt. His eyes went toward the

rear of the kitchen, where silhouettes of feces stains were still on the wall. "He's...downstairs."

Matt and Crash traded glances.

Crash leaned across the table. "Repeat that."

Campbell said, "He's downstairs."

Campbell led Matt and Crash downstairs into an unfinished basement. There were plastic storage boxes stacked against the concrete wall, black garbage bags, a washer and dryer, and power tools scattered across the floor.

Campbell pointed toward the far wall and let himself drop onto one of the plastic boxes. "He's in there."

Matt placed his hands on his waist as he stared at the concrete.

"Tyson Miller is in the wall," Matt said.

Campbell nodded and buried his face into his age-rattled hands.

Matt heaved a deep breath. "Goddamn but this got gothic out of nowhere, didn't it?"

Crash stepped up next to Matt. "I feel like we've officially hit the point where this is bigger than us."

"I can call in the dayside guys. They won't like it, but they'll like the overtime pay."

"I don't mean *us* as in you and me. This is bigger than the department."

"Then what are you suggesting?" Each word dropped slowly, with intention.

Crash let her silence answer the question. Matt knew.

"No," he said. "No fucking way."

"We have to. We're not equipped for this kind of shit. We don't have another choice."

Matt grimaced. "I'm going to fucking hate myself for this."

Chapter 28

"Jesus Christ," Jackie Hall said. "This all took a turn, didn't it?"

"That it did," Matt said. They stood in the basement next to one another as two state troopers, stripped down to T-shirts and gray uniform pants, respirators pulled over their faces, took swings at the concrete wall. As cracks and gaps appeared, they used crowbars and hammers and chisels to pull away the loosened pieces before going back to swinging.

Matt called Jackie out of sheer reluctance. Crash was right. This was bigger than the sheriff's department could handle alone, and calling the state police was the only sane option. The dings to Matt's pride didn't matter; he knew this wasn't the time for a dick-measuring contest.

The two men stood shoulder to shoulder, arms crossed, with their own respirators draped around their necks and hanging against their chests. Crime scene tape had been put up, and they watched from the other side, out of reach of concrete dust.

"The robberies were all men who belonged to the Benevolent Order," Jackie Hall said.

"That's what Campbell said."

"Goddamn. My old man, he belonged to that group when I was a kid. All I ever remember them doing was raising money for cancer and driving those little cars in parades, wearing funny hats."

"I suspect the national charter didn't sanction the bank robberies."

"I don't suppose they did." Jackie Hall shook his head. "What's going on in the world to have shit like this happening?"

"Can't blame this on now. You're talking almost twenty years ago. Not the same place now it was then. It was changing then too. This has nothing to do with the world. This is all people. People and greed. Not accepting that the world's not what it was for their fathers and grandfathers."

Jackie Hall looked down and saw the dust piling up on his shoes. He took a step back and observed the clean space on the floor where his feet had been. He looked back to the demolition work. "What's your problem with me?"

Neither man said anything for a moment. Jackie said, "I've been in Parker County a fair number of years now, and you and I come across each other regular enough, and I try to be the best sort of person I can be. But every time you see me, you act like you caught me pissing in your pool. Can't help but say it feels somewhat passive-aggressive."

Matt laughed. "Passive-aggressive? Really?"

"My wife teaches elementary school, and passive-aggressive is the default mode for most of her students."

"You comparing me to grade school kids?"

"If the shoe fits."

"Fair enough. I suppose if I've got to be honest, Lieutenant—"

"See, it's that right there. 'Lieutenant' I ask you every time to stop calling me that, to call me Jackie, and you keep on calling me Lieutenant."

"Okay then, Jackie, if you're asking me to be honest, then no, I don't like you much. By now, I'm not sure how much of it is you and how much of it is the amount of grudge I've built up against you over the years."

"Would you mind sharing with me what I've done to earn that hostility? Because while there's plenty of people I work overtime on making miserable, I doubt I've ever said a harsh word to you."

"You've done nothing, Jackie. That's the damn thing, is you've done nothing. All these years, you've been nothing but courteous and professional. You don't walk into our cases swinging your dick, wanting to take things over, acting like we're nothing but a bunch of rubes and imbeciles."

"You run a clean department, with a good closure rate. Not much reason to tread into your jurisdiction without a need. Then what is it?"

"I guess if I have to narrow it down to something, it's that everything just fucking seems to work out for you."

Jackie twisted his head to stare at Matt. He furrowed his brow, the skin on his forehead rolling on top of one another into folds. Matt stared straight ahead at the wall.

"I suppose you heard about me having cancer," he said.

"I've heard things."

"Then you know there's a good likelihood I'm not long for this world. I'm the black banana of the local law enforcement community. Which blows, because on any other scale, I'm not doing too bad. But my wife will end up a widow much, much sooner than I ever expected. Plus, we never got to have kids. I wanted them but she didn't, and once we divorced, I gave up on all of that. By the time we got back together and things found that equilibrium again, the doctors told me I was sucking down on 'The Big C,' which sounds way more sexual than I had intended it to. Moving on.

"You, though. We keep on dealing and meeting with one another, and your life seems great. You're good at your job. You've got a wife and family and they seem to love you. Your life, Jackie, is good. It's the life I dreamed about when I was in the army in Germany busting drunk grunts. All I wanted was to come back to Parker County and settle down and live out my life, peaceful and quiet, with Rachel and a passel of kids who'd hate me when they were teenagers, then someday give me grandchildren. But that's not the plan the universe worked out for me. Call it God or Mother Nature or whatever you opt to term it—

it all decided that I'd be better off with liver cancer. The entire time I've known you, my life has been in one form of disintegration or another. You, on the other hand, seem to be infinitely blessed. And no, I would never want anything to happen to you or your family. But I suppose I'd like a smidge of the luck you seem to have. If you wouldn't mind sharing some of that with me, I'd be grateful."

Again, they fell into silence, all except for the steady pounding of the sledgehammers smashing the wall into chunks. They stood there without another word, the dust swirling around them.

A deputy was ready to take a swing when another deputy held his hand up, stopping him, and peeked into the growing hole in the wall. He pulled his head back and pulled off his respirator and gagged a little. Took a deep breath and said, "Lieutenant! Sheriff! You'll wanna get a look at this."

Matt and Jackie stepped underneath the yellow crime scene tape. Jackie yelled to a trooper to turn one of the work lights around toward the hole.

The smell caught up to them before they saw it. Maybe *it* wasn't the right way to phrase what was there, but Matt couldn't think of any other way to describe it. What stared back at them had been human once upon a time, but that time had worn it down to nothing but bone and ragged bits of flesh. The skull hung loose on the body, as if the slightest movement might snap it free. A small dark hole rested in the middle of the skull's forehead. A cockroach, large and glistening in the light, skittered out of an empty eye socket and down into the mouth, vanishing into the gaping maw. Clothing had mostly rotted away or melded to the bone and fleshy tendrils, making it hard to know where anything began or ended.

But Jesus, the smell that smacked both men hard was heavy and putrid—a sweet yet sour stink, a stench that obliterated the all-too-familiar smell of bloated, rotting roadkill in the summer sun, or the occasional corpse found locked up in a house for weeks on end, left to stew and fester in its own literal juices.

THE RIGHTEOUS PATH

No, this was a new kind of foul—something that neither man was ready for. This was what *dead* smelled like. Dead in the worst way imaginable. Dead without dignity or formality. The smell of twenty years spent hidden away, now released into the world. They had, until that moment, thought they knew what that smell was, and right then and there they understood they hadn't known shit.

Jackie lost it first. He turned his head and puked, the splattering against the ground like someone dumped a bucket of chunky soup across concrete. There went the fried chicken he had at lunch, the bag of Fritos he ate while filling out evaluations in the afternoon, the roast beef and potatoes at dinner, the two slices of chocolate cake for dessert, both Snickers bars he'd eaten on the drive out to the crime scene...all of it right there for everyone to see.

Matt made it to the other side of the tape and across the room to a small garbage can that had already been there. His day had been lighter—a sandwich at lunch, tilapia Rachel had made for dinner, ice cream—and it took less time to void his gullet. He was more accustomed to vomiting than Jackie was, he suspected. Such was the beauty of cancer.

The police around watched and said nothing and waited for it to be done so they could go back to work. They'd probably talk about it later. But for now, nothing but the sound of puking. That sound rattled between the walls.

Chapter 29

Jackie and Matt came upstairs from the basement and walked into the kitchen. Crash sat at the table with Campbell. She looked at the men. Both chewed gum like their lives depended on it.

To Matt, she said, "You got any more gum?"

Matt shook his head. "I need all I've got."

She shifted her gaze from Matt to Jackie. "You?"

"Sorry," Jackie said. "I'm working the half of the pack he gave me."

Her eyes darted back and forth between the two men. A thin gauze of sweat covered their faces.

"You both look like you're on the wrong side of death's door," she said.

Matt lifted his eyebrows.

Crash shrugged. "Poor choice of words. You okay?"

Matt said, "I'm gonna say I've been better."

"Was Miller down there?"

Jackie nodded. "He most definitely was."

Matt pulled a chair away from the table and sat across from Campbell. Leaned in close to the old man.

"There's a bullet hole in the middle of his forehead," Matt said.

Campbell nodded. "Yes."

"I'm not asking for confirmation; I'm stating as fact. What I want is for you to tell me how it got there, because I'll bet Miller didn't put it there himself."

Campbell's chest rose and fell with a heaving breath. "Roger killed him."

Jackie moved in closer. "Roger Waits, who happens to be dead?"

Matt settled back in his chair. "Jesus. That's convenient as hell, isn't it? Waits is dead, so he can't defend himself. But the problem becomes how the dead body is in your house—walled up in your basement, even. Before you tell me more about how Roger killed Miller, I need you to consider that there are zero reasons to believe you, how the Feds will show up in a few hours and bury you underneath a literal shit-ton of federal charges, and compound it all with you being older than shit on the underside of a rock. You may as well make the choice to be honest about this because lying won't do a goddamn thing about the prison time you're facing. What it will do is be one less thing to tick off your conscience before you meet your maker."

Campbell sat upright and planted his palms flat on his legs. What Matt saw in that moment was a man resigned to his fate, who, in a flash, made his peace with the world. "No chance of going easy on an old man?"

"None whatsoever."

"I had to make the effort," Campbell said. "After the second robbery—after Roger shot that girl—we met back at one of Pete's work sites. Everyone was on edge. We all yelled at Roger, and Roger was pissed off because we were mad at him. Murdering that girl didn't bother him. He kept saying he had saved us because the dye pack would have ruined the money and the whole thing would have been for nothing." Campbell shook his head. "Those years I'd known Roger, he'd never been what you'd call a compassionate soul—he was the last to volunteer to ring the bell at Christmas every year—but whatever had been in him died then and there."

"About the corpse in your basement," Matt said.

"I'm getting there. Anyway, we were angry, but Tyson was

furious. Told Roger he should have stayed in the car, that he had no business trying to make something like this work from the inside. He and Roger got into a tussle—"

"A tussle?" Jackie said. "Like pushing each other around?"

"Yes. It didn't seem like anything serious, and we tried to break it up, but then Roger landed a punch right to Tyson's jaw, and everything flipped. You know, the life Tyson lived, he'd been in fights, he knew how to handle himself, and Roger was nothing but a guy who'd spent his life pushing money from one column to another. But he was doing so much coke, he was a wild man. Tyson snapped and got Roger square in the nose. It shattered Roger's nose, and blood poured down his face. Tyson stepped back, Roger wiped blood away, and then he had a gun in his hand, and—"

"Roger shot Tyson," Matt said.

"Right in the head," Campbell said. "The hole in front, it wasn't much, but the back of his skull shattered, and the mess splattered everywhere. The floor, the walls. It took hours to clean it up."

Matt's right hand curled into a fist then relaxed. Again and again. "That mess had a wife and a baby on the way, Mr. Campbell."

"I didn't kill him, Sheriff. I swear on my darling Wilma's life. Roger pulled a pistol and shot Tyson. He did it like it was nothing too. If I could have stopped him, I would have. That's the truth, Sheriff. When this started, no one was supposed to get hurt."

Matt exhaled through his nose and ran his hands through his hair, rubbing his head then patting his hair back into place. Such a long fucking night.

Jackie crossed his arms over his chest, letting them rest on his gut, and leaned back against the wall. "How'd it become a good idea, you stick the body in your basement?"

Campbell shifted in his seat. "No one had a clue what to do with it. We could have poured him into concrete at one of Roger's projects, except business was as dead as Miller was. We thought about burying him out in the woods, but we worried someone going squirrel hunting would be out there and their dog would luck along and dig him up. But I was having the basement worked on, and I said we could just put him in the wall. We wrapped him in a tarp, brought him back here. We threw quicklime on him to keep the smell down, and then everyone helped me dodge up a new wall. The space was small enough, Wilma never noticed the difference. She didn't care so long as the washer and dryer kept on working."

Jackie held up an open palm. "Stop for a minute. You had a dead body in your basement for almost twenty years. Fine. I've got that part of things. What about the money? What happened to it?"

"It's gone," Campbell said. "We split it. Everyone got their shares, and I don't know what they did with it."

Matt said, "But when the people attacked you in your house, they asked you for the money from the Guthrie job, didn't they?"

"Yes."

"And you didn't tell us because you knew it might tie you back to the robberies, and to the murders."

"I'm an old man, Sheriff. There's not much more left in my world. I had Wilma, but the doctors asked me today how long I want to keep her on life support. My daughter, she walked away from me years ago. Whoever's doing this, they've taken goddamn near everything I've got, and telling you the truth didn't seem the best way to keep what I had for the time I have left."

Matt looked back at Jackie. "Can you get your guys in here to keep an eye on Mr. Campbell, and the three of us step out for a few?"

Campbell said, "How many do you need to keep me in here? Do you imagine I'll try to make a run for it?"

"Don't know. Hadn't expected to be excavating a corpse out

of a basement wall, Mr. Campbell, so who knows what the hell else the night holds?"

Chapter 30

On the front porch, Matt did some deep knee bends and stretched his arms out. He felt tight and coiled and needed something to loosen those parts of him. He debated sending one of his deputies out to get coffee. He thought it may have violated an unknown precedent or protocol to make a pot from Campbell's kitchen. He would have made it himself, though. He was okay with coffee from Campbell's house so long as it came on his terms.

Jackie Hall scratched at his head and stared at the swirling kaleidoscope of lights in the driveway. State police. Sheriff's department. The medical examiner's van pulled in behind the others. He took a deep, heavy breath and noticed Crash had stepped off the porch, onto the front lawn's deep green grass.

"You're sure it's Miller's daughter and the McCoy boy behind the home invasions and the explosion at the flower shop?" Jackie said.

"About as sure as you can be about anything, circumstances such as this," Matt said.

"What do you think happens, we take Campbell in?"

"The way the universe works, he'll probably die before he ever sees trial for the laundry list of charges stacking up against him. An orange jumpsuit will be the last suit of clothes he ever wears. His wife is going to die. We can write off arresting Carlton because he's never going to wake up."

"And what about the Miller girl and the McCoy boy?"

"On that, I'm fucking clueless. Seems like they figured they could get money out of these guys. Somehow she figured out shit no one else did for twenty years. Maybe she thought she was owed her father's share." He shook his head. "Kids don't realize life is a zero-sum game. No matter how we play it, the score's the same in the end."

"You that much of a pessimist, Sheriff?"

"People call it pessimism when they don't want to admit the facts. Everyone loses in this one."

"I don't call it losing when we close the books on something like this."

"Book's not closed yet. We still have to find Micki Miller and Billy McCoy. Besides, I'm curious still how they put together what the Feds couldn't."

Crash came back up onto the porch. "We could go ahead and call the news. Give them a heads-up early in the game. There's not going to be bigger news than finding a two-decade-old corpse tied to a series of previously unsolved bank robberies. Everyone in town will talk it up."

Matt gave a nod of understanding. "Which means Micki and Billy will hear about it."

"Same songbook, boss."

"Flush them out that way?" Jackie said.

"It'll push them to realize they don't have any other plays left," Matt said. "I'll call up the *Herald-Tribune* editor, tell him what's happening. That pushes the story out early, and let the dominos fall from there."

Crash exchanged glances with the two men. "Anyone else got a better idea?"

"I got nothing," Matt said.

"Snake eyes here," Jackie said.

Crash smiled. "Jesus but I fucking love being the smartest person in the room."

"We're outside, Crash."

"Let me have this moment, Matt."

By 9 a.m., it was the buzz of Serenity. When the lunchtime rush hit O'Dell's, the courthouse office workers were all talking about it. The Clarksburg stations picked it up off the *Herald-Tribune* website and sent out broadcast vans and reporters to do live remotes outside the courthouse. It was the biggest small-market news to hit since the National Brotherhood stir-up. When the news outlets called the sheriff's department and the state police, all they got was "No comment" and "This is part of an ongoing investigation, and we'll release information as it becomes available."

Matt went home and went to bed. Rachel was gone by the time he got there. The bed had been made, of course, because that was who Rachel was, and he almost felt bad for disturbing it. Everything had been tucked and settled perfectly.

He ran his shower as hot as he could stand until his skin felt ready to blister and peel. He scrubbed and rinsed and scrubbed again, working to pull off the sticky sweet smell of decay from the basement. Afterward, he pulled the covers aside and climbed in naked and—in spite of the coffee and pizza rolls rolling around inside his system—fell asleep as his head hit the pillow.

Chapter 31

Rachel came home to find her husband naked and snoring in bed, and she undressed and slid in next to him, nuzzling as close to him as she could. She worked not to think what it would be like for this to be gone. Her marriage to the attorney hadn't been like this. There'd been nothing sweet or comfortable in it. She was never certain what she had seen in him except that he was there, present and interested and offered an attention to her Matt wasn't offering. Which led to a guilt she carried more than she cared to admit, either to herself or to Matt.

There had been Matt—a good man, yes, but always working, never letting go of those years he'd spent in the army, regimented and conditioned by that life. And, if she was honest with herself, a sheriff's salary, plus his military retirement—even in Parker County—didn't give her a life she wanted.

Christ. She hated that. The shame of choosing someone else, someone lesser. She tried not to dwell on time lost, on the ticking clock inside of Matt gnawing away at the minutes and hours they had. He was probably convinced she ignored the problem, the reality of it all—of the cancer—because she didn't want to talk about it for so long. Actually, the thoughts about it had consumed her, and now when she tried to get him to talk about the cancer, he refused. Like he was protecting her, keeping her safe. Another Matt trait that drove her insane.

All that happened was she kept reminding herself that she

would wake up one day, on a day like this, and he wouldn't be there. Not an unfamiliar experience, sure. But it was knowing that the next morning, he wouldn't be there, either. Or any other mornings. The bed would be big and empty, and the pillowcases wouldn't smell like his drugstore aftershave, and she would reach out for him for all of those future mornings and keep on reaching and reaching for something that would never be there again.

Matt woke up around six. Rachel stared at him, naked, smiling. Without a word, she kissed him, her hand slipping underneath the sheets and grabbing him, teasing him until he was ready, and she rolled him onto his back and climbed on top of him. She did all the work, feeling him, all of him, his rough hands against her smooth skin, holding on to her, subtly trying to shift control.

She resisted his efforts to slow her down, to steady her. She leaned forward and pushed the flats of her hands on his chest and forced him deeper into her. Her eyes locked on him, a sly little smile on her face. He couldn't help but smile himself, and when he reached up to kiss her, she pushed him back down and laid a finger across his lips and said, "No."

He lost himself in this moment, as he did with all his moments with Rachel, in this rapture he wanted to make last forever. Not out of pride, out of boasting, out of something to show off, but because he hated the thought of letting her go.

When they finished, sore and sweaty and the sheets soaked, Matt stared upward at the ceiling and blinked.

"Goddamn," he said.

She leaned over and stretched her arm across his chest. "Gonna live?"

"Yes." He pulled her closer. "I am."

He cooked steaks on the grill, along with potatoes and corn. It was early in the season, but he didn't care. Matt fired up the grill in January with snow on the ground simply because he wanted to. A charcoal grill. Always charcoal, never gas.

After eating, as they drank their tea, he told her about Campbell and what had happened, with the sun moving deeper in the sky and making beautiful everything the violet light touched.

"What about the kids? They started all of this?" she said.

"That's how it looks," Matt said. "We're hoping since there's no one left to pay them now, they'll turn themselves in."

"All of this was for nothing but money?"

"Money or revenge or both. I find that in life, those are often motivating factors whenever someone chooses to do something ugly."

"How did she know her father was involved? Or that Campbell and the others were part of the robberies?"

"That's the question I'll ask when I catch her." He set his glass aside and looked out across the yard. "She's seventeen. The boyfriend's not much older. All of this damage and chaos, and neither one of them old enough to know what the hell they're doing."

"People older than them have done more."

"They have, but they had the years of life wearing them down, making them angry and bitter. If you're this way at that age, there's not much in the world that'll make it better for you. That's the thing with the world is that you can't act like it's supposed to be fair or right, and I get the sense what these two were looking for was a way to right a wrong, to make things fair. That whole thing about two wrongs trying to equal a right."

Rachel reached over and set her hand on top of his. "You'll get them."

Matt twisted his hand around and let his fingers spider about Rachel's hand, and he savored the soft warmth of his wife's touch.

Chapter 32

The phone rang as they got ready for bed.

Rachel stared at the device as it buzzed on the bedside. The night had been quiet, and it had made her ponder what life might be like once Matt wasn't the sheriff anymore. After the cancer, and finding themselves starting over again. A real new beginning, away from Parker County.

Matt sat on the edge of the bed as he reached for the phone. Rachel touched his shoulder.

"Deal with it in the morning," she said.

"It's the office," he said. "If they're calling me this late—"

"They always call this late. It's Crash or the office or the state police or—"

Matt answered the phone. It was Will Mitchell, who worked night dispatch.

"Sheriff, I'm sorry to be calling you but—"

"It's fine, Will. What's up?"

"Iris Warner's been calling all evening, said she needed to talk to you. I tried to give her your cell number—where it's on your business cards, I know you don't mind—but she said she wanted to speak to you directly. In my mind, there's nothing more direct than her calling your cell phone, though. Unless she wants to send you a singing telegram."

Matt knew he had given Iris a business card. It felt odd she hadn't simply called him. His phone had sat silent all night. Not even a text from Crash, checking in on him. He had appreciated the break.

Matt said thanks and ended the call and sat up in bed, swinging his feet over onto the floor.

"Where are you going?" Rachel said.

He walked to the closet and shuffled through his clothing. "Something's weird, and I can't put my finger on what it is. I'm going to head out and check on it."

"That's the absolute vaguest thing I've ever heard in my life, Matthew Simms."

Matt pulled a sheriff's department polo shirt over his head, tucking the tail into his blue jeans. He reached up onto a shelf and brought out a lock box, tapped the code into the keypad to open it, and removed a 9 mm pistol and holster.

"It won't take long," he said. He snapped the pistol and holster to his belt. "It's the Campbell thing, that's all."

"Did they find the two kids?"

"No. I suspect the kids found something, though."

Matt pulled his car out of the garage and onto the street, Rachel watching him through the living room window. Even in the darkness he could see her face, or he imagined he could—coiled frustration she wore like a mask.

At a stoplight, he called Iris's phone. When she answered, her voice sounded taut and nervous but struggling to seem natural and relaxed.

"Sheriff?" she said.

"Ms. Warner. Understand you've been trying to get in touch with me."

"Yes. I need to get in contact with my father."

"Well, he's at the North Central Regional Jail in Sutton. You'll have to call and set up an appointment for visitation."

"This is urgent, Sheriff. I have to speak with him now."

Matt was ten minutes from Warner's hotel in Serenity. Moving his eyes back and forth from the road to his phone, he switched to the texting app, found Crash's number, and moved his thumb across the keyboard.

Meet me at the Wiltshire. Now.

To Iris, he said, "Everything okay, Ms. Warner?"

"Yes. But I've been seeing all of this on the news, and I had no idea about any of it"—Iris's voice strained to stress the last part—"and this matter is urgent. You know how much I care about my father, Sheriff."

"I'm well aware of your feelings for your father, Ms. Warner."

The messaging app on Matt's phone beeped.

Crash: *What's up?*

Matt: *Something with Iris Warner. I'll explain there. Park down the street. Don't bring a cruiser.*

He paused and wondered if he needed to tell her to carry a gun. He didn't. She would anyway.

Iris said, "Is there anything you can do for me, Sheriff?"

"I'll see what I can make happen."

"Thank you, Sheriff."

The line went dead, and Matt cast the phone into the passenger seat.

Crash parked her pickup—one of the ugliest vehicles Matt had seen in a life filled with views of the various atrocities committed against the vehicular gods—three blocks down from the Wiltshire. He pulled up behind her and met her on the sidewalk. She wore a WVU T-shirt and blue jeans and a .45 clipped to her belt.

He told her about the phone call. "Now I'm thinking maybe Micki Miller and Billy McCoy found Iris Warner, and they're holding her in her hotel room."

"You got all of that from one phone call?"

"Iris doesn't need to come to me to get in contact with her father. Besides, she could have called me herself at any point.

Her making me call her was supposed to mean something. To convey an urgency."

"Should we call Jackie Hall?"

Matt shook his head. "Jackie'll want to bring in a SWAT-type unit, and it'll raise ruckus and fuss before there's an opportunity to act. If they're in there, Miller and McCoy—"

"Key is *if*," Crash said.

"If they're in there, they have a tendency toward staggering acts of violence. They see something that seems off, they won't have a problem doing something stupid."

"So we're doing something stupid in their stead?"

"I suppose we are."

"Is every boss like you?"

"How many bosses have you had in your life?"

"Other than working at Walmart in college? Just you."

"Damn. I hadn't realized what a high bar I was setting for everyone else to have to clear."

"You keep thinking that. I'm gonna get my vest out of the truck."

"You keep your body armor in your personal vehicle?"

"No, I keep the vest I bought in my personal vehicle. The one the county issued me, that's in the cruiser." She smiled. "I like to be prepared."

Chapter 33

The lobby was empty. This late at night, Matt expected it to be. Truth be told, he hoped for it. The fewer people who saw them, the better.

A guy snored in a chair inside the lobby entrance. "Passed out" was the better term. Matt could smell him from five feet away, a combination of alcohol sweats and filth. He sprawled out across a threadbare green chair, wearing grease-stained Dickies and a T-shirt that read "Fuck Me, I'm Irish." A small yellow puddle encircled the floor around his right foot.

The guy working the front desk stared at Matt and Crash with wide-eyed concern as they crossed the lobby floor, Matt resting his hand on his gun and Crash dressed in body armor that doubled her size, holding a pump-action shotgun at her side.

The clerk was retirement age, with a ring of white hair wrapped around a liver-spotted skull. He wore a faded blue dress shirt and a stained tie and a business-like facade that felt overdone for the surroundings. He nodded toward Matt as Matt smiled at him and checked his name badge. Walt.

"Sheriff," the clerk said. "What can I help you with this evening?"

"You've got a guest on the sixth floor, room 612. Is there anyone on either side of her, Walt?"

Walt adjusted the wire-rimmed glasses on his face and leaned over the counter closer to Matt. "What's this about, Sheriff? What's Ms. Warner done?"

"Ms. Warner's not done anything. But there could be something wrong and we need to know there's not anyone in those rooms."

Walt turned his attention to a computer behind the counter and tapped on the keyboard. "Rooms 610 and 614 are both vacant." He swung his gaze back to Matt. His eyes moved over to Crash and the shotgun. "I'm sorry, Sheriff, but what exactly is going on here that requires you coming in *armed*?" He emphasized the last word.

Matt brought his phone out of his pocket and flipped through it. "How long have you been on duty tonight?"

"Since about six. Why?"

Matt spun his phone around and showed Walt a photo of Micki. "This girl look familiar to you? Have you seen her tonight?"

"Not that I can recall, no."

Matt slid his thumb across the screen and brought up a photo of Billy. "What about him?"

Walt focused on the picture as though struggling to recall a terrible wrong from the past. "I think I saw him come in earlier this evening. He stuck out somewhat, since he's young and we don't get many young people coming through here." He rubbed at his chin. "The girl from that first picture, she might have been with him. He came in with someone. They walked in, went straight to the elevator, and that was that."

"What about Iris Warner? Have you seen or talked to her tonight?"

"Not tonight, no. We've spoken before, when she asked about places to eat, things like that." Walt stood up straight. "Again, Sheriff, I need to ask what's happening here. Is this something that will put our other guests at risk?"

Crash cocked an eyebrow. "How many guests you got tonight?"

Walt looked hurt by Crash's tone, as though she had insulted his pride. "Enough that the possibility of violence is a concern, regardless of the number."

"You mean like when we busted the meth lab on the fifth floor?" Crash said. "Wait. There was the one on five, then the one on the second floor." She ticked off numbers on her fingers. "How many times was this? Two, three, four—"

Matt sighed. He grabbed Crash's wrist and gave it a gentle squeeze. She froze and dropped her hands to her side as he let go.

Matt said, "Walt, you've got a job to do, and so do we, and keeping everyone safe is our first concern, which is why there's only the two of us. Ms. Warner could be in danger, and so we're going to go up on six and see what we can do about that. Now you said the rooms on the other sides of her are empty. How's the rest of the floor look?"

"It's empty," Walt said. "Ms. Warner is the only occupant on the floor."

Crash said, "Why's that? Are the other floors booked?"

"No," Walt said. His face flushed again, but it was a gradual sense of embarrassment. "We're having the other floors renovated."

"Aren't those the floors where we found the meth labs?"

Matt kicked at Crash. He hit her in the calf, and she muttered something angrily under her breath.

"Do you have a master key for the rooms?" Matt said. "So we can get into 610 or 614?"

Walt opened a drawer underneath the counter and rummaged through until he found a small ring of keys. He pulled one key free and handed it to Matt.

"We'll be moving everything over to the electronic card readers like other hotels in the next phase of renovations, but for now, we're old-fashioned, I suppose," he said.

Matt wrapped his hand around the key and smiled. "Thanks for your help, Walt. Now we're going to head on upstairs. I need you not to say or do anything while we're up there. Don't call your boss, don't order takeout from the Riverside, don't roust awake the guy asleep over there, anything like that. We need you to be as quiet and low-key as possible so we can be as quiet and low-key as possible. Can you do that for us?"

Walt nodded.

"Much appreciated," Matt said as he and Crash headed for the elevator.

Matt reached for the elevator call button. Crash swatted his hand away and pressed the button.

"Your people skills suck," Matt said.

Crash shrugged and whistled, swinging the shotgun back and forth in her hand.

"Why aren't you wearing body armor?" she said.

"Because if what I think is waiting for us actually is, looking like I came to fight won't do anything but stir the pot. Besides, what are the odds it'll be bullets that kill me?"

Crash shook her head. "You've got to lay off the cancer jokes, dude," she said as the elevator doors slid open.

They rode the elevator to the fifth floor, then took the stairs up to six. Matt pushed the bar to open the stairwell door with the butt of Crash's shotgun, cracking it enough for him to peek his head out.

"Anyone out there?" Crash said.

Matt drew himself back into the stairwell and held onto the door as it closed, the click barely above a whisper.

"Seems they are not, since no one shot at me," Matt said.

Crash unwrapped a stick of gum and tossed it in her mouth. "Are you legit this worried about the possibility of two kids?"

"They're kids with nothing to lose, Crash. They either think they'll live forever or they don't care if they don't. Either way, based on the past week, caution is the right way to go here."

Crash blew a bubble and let it pop. "Okay, boss. I'll let you take the lead."

Chapter 34

Matt knocked on Iris's room door. He leaned in close to the wood and heard what sounded like several people moving without grace, knocking into furniture in hurried and awkward movements. Hushed voices, shuffled footsteps, muttered curses, the rattle and clicking of the door's locks being unfastened, and the door opening wide enough to allow a wedge of light to shine out from the room. Matt saw a sliver of Iris's face. Her eyes were large, the pupils small, her mouth drawn into a tight O.

"Sheriff," she said. "Rather late for you to be out, isn't it?"

Matt gave his best smile. "I had a few questions, and I hoped we could talk."

"You caught me as I was heading to bed. I need to get up early and try to talk to my father in the morning."

"About that. My understanding is the Feds are picking him up about six and heading him up to Pittsburgh to talk about the bank robberies."

Iris gave a small but audible gasp. "Um, Sheriff, I've got to get a hold of him. This is…this is important. It's…"

"I'm sorry, Ms. Warner, but it's all above my pay grade. Once the Feds lay their hands on him, then he's not going anywhere or talking to anyone who's not his lawyer for a while."

Iris's eyes darted to the side, and her hand reached out and took hold of the door. She trembled like she was struggling to stand. Her voice cracked.

The door flew open wide and someone pushed Iris out of the way and the next thing Matt saw was Billy McCoy pointing a gun in his face. Matt stood motionless, hands to his side, staring down at the barrel of the pistol. It was less than a foot from his face, a .38 caliber, snub-nosed, gleaming in the light. It looked well taken care of, and Matt could smell the gun oil, which meant a recent cleaning. So Billy liked the gun and respected it and knew how to use it. It implied Billy might be a decent shot—not that it was a concern at less than a foot—and he also may not have a problem pulling the trigger. Nausea swelled and churned in Matt's stomach. For all his talk of being unafraid of death, this wasn't how he wanted shit to go down. Not that he had preferences about how to die—not that he wanted to die at all—but he knew for certain he didn't want to get shot in the face and left to bleed out in the lobby of a shitty hotel.

A bead of sweat dripped from Matt's forehead and across his eye. The salt burned and made his eye water, and he squinted to keep his focus on Billy and the gun. Billy kept his aim steady on Matt. Finger on the trigger, ready to fire if he didn't like the way things looked. Attention square and sure on Matt. No emotion on his face. He was bigger than the pictures had implied. Time spent at the gym. He had bulk and muscle and youth all on Matt. Plus, there was the gun. Matt's gun, still holstered, mattered damn little at the moment.

Behind Billy, from somewhere toward the back of the room, a woman's voice said, "Goddamn, Billy, get him in here."

"Micki?" Matt said. "Micki Miller?"

Micki stepped out to where Matt could see her. Her face was hard and angry, and she didn't look like the girl Matt had seen in the photos. She had taken on a focus, a determination, that skated on the edge of dangerous. She clutched a pistol in her right hand. Matt guessed she wasn't a little girl anymore.

Matt said, "Your mother's worried about you, Micki. She's been looking for you. She's had me and my deputies looking for you."

Micki walked closer to the door. Billy kept his ground, motionless. That was when Matt realized where Iris was: on the ground, trembling as though the floor shook underneath her.

Micki came up behind Iris, grabbed her by the hair, and yanked her to her feet. Iris yelped like a whipped puppy. Micki twisted Iris's hair around her hand while pushing her pistol underneath the woman's chin.

"How is Mom?" Micki asked. Her eyes were as dead and flat as a doll's eyes. "She good? What about the boys? How are her precious boys?" She pulled Iris back. To Billy, she said, "Get him the fuck in here."

Billy said, "You heard the lady. Move your ass."

Matt stepped into the hotel room. Billy moved over to let him in, closing the door behind him, clicking the locks once the door was secure, never letting the barrel of his pistol get very far from Matt's head.

Micki led Iris over to a couch and slung her onto it. Iris slammed into the furniture with force and melted into its shape.

Billy held out his free hand. "Hand it over." Matt unclipped the holster from his belt and handed it to him. Billy motioned toward the table. "Get comfortable."

Matt sized up the situation. Micki was about two feet from Iris, with her gun trained on her. Billy stood at the far end of the table, gun pointed at Matt.

Matt took a seat at the table, rested his arms on the table top. "This isn't the only play to this. You can let her go, and we can all go over to the courthouse and settle things up, and no one gets hurt."

"We all know that's not true, and it's not happening, Sheriff," Micki said. "Shit's not settled until those bastards pay me what I'm owed."

"Tell me what you think you're owed, Micki."

"Well, those bank robberies scored them all about, what?

More than a million dollars, right?"

"Close to a million and a half."

"And what they should have done was split that money up five ways. That would have given my daddy about a quarter-million dollars, right?"

"Sounds about right."

"What's the phrase the lawyers use, honey?"

"Pain and suffering," Billy said. He said it without inflection. He seemed bored by the whole thing, as though hostage-taking wasn't enough to keep his interest.

"Pain and suffering," Micki repeated. "These fuckers owe me for pain and suffering. So what'll happen is that Campbell's gonna shit out that money—him and the rest of those fuckers—or I'll scatter his daughter's brains out all over the wall."

"Campbell's in jail, Micki," Matt said. "The other one you attacked, he's still in a coma. Two of them are already dead. And that money is long gone, spent years ago. All that's left is old men waiting to die."

"No," Micki said. She shook her head as if trying to make Matt's words go away. "Campbell's got money. I know he's rich. He owned all those grocery stores. You don't do that and not be rich."

"He robbed those banks because he was broke. The stores were going under, and he borrowed from loan sharks he couldn't pay back. There's nothing left."

"Bullshit," Micki said. "He's got money somewhere. He's driving a fucking Cadillac. Don't tell me he's broke."

Iris pulled her knees up close to her chest and wrapped her arms around her legs. Fresh bruises had formed on her face, ripening and taking color.

A sigh sounded from Matt. "Okay, let's say Campbell's got money. Doesn't change there's no way of getting to him. The Feds will lay hands on him like it's Sunday morning, and they're not letting go. How much ransom money you think you can milk from a man in federal prison orange?"

"This ain't ransom money," Micki said. "I'm owed this. This money is mine. They took my daddy from me. Ain't I owed something for that?"

"You're nothing but a kid, Micki, and I know the world looks this one particular way to you, but let me share a secret with you I had to learn the hard way: the universe owes you jack." He shifted his gaze from Billy to her. "Whatever they've told you in school, or you read in books, or preachers yelled at you, it's bullshit. The universe has zero fucks to offer you. You're owed nothing, and nothing is owed to you. You and the boyfriend over there bandying about Parker County, blowing shit up and whatnot, won't make the universe change its plans, because there are no plans."

Micki stepped up behind Billy and laid her hand on his shoulder. He reached up and took her hand.

"So be it," she said. "But I ain't asking anything from the universe. I'm asking it from men who killed my father."

Matt slouched in his chair, relaxing into its shape. It was easier than it should have been, what with a pair of JV-squad psychos pointing guns at him.

"How did you connect your father to these men and the robberies?" he said. "You managed something an awful lot of cops weren't able to do."

Micki smiled, a shy, bashful grin that offered a reminder she was still seventeen. "Wasn't much detective work, Sheriff. Mom sent me out into the storage building one day to find papers she needed for something, and there pushed to the back was a cardboard box I'd guess we've moved from every shithole apartment, trailer, and house we've been in over the years. I opened it and dug in and realized it was from before I was born, and it was stuff from my dad. Pictures of him and my mom, and pictures of him with his people. Car parts and notebooks and random things Mom shoved into a box after he disappeared, but she never got rid of because...because they were his. Something I found was a spiral-bound notebook, and the handwriting wasn't like Mom's, so it had to be Dad's. Didn't seem like anything but random lists. Movies they'd seen together, and books he'd read, and baby names—"

"Baby names for you, I'd bet."

"Yeah. Anyway, midway through I found this stack of paperback books. They were all yellowed and old, and they all looked like total guy shit, with chicks with big tits and men with guns and all that crap. The descriptions on the back, they were all about bank robberies."

Matt jerked his head in Billy's direction. "We found them at his place."

Micki looked at Billy. "We shouldn't have kept them there."

Billy shrugged. "I was reading them."

Micki turned back to Matt. "When I flipped through the pages on one, a business card dropped out for that florist shop in town. Then I saw on the inside cover of one Daddy had written a bunch of names, and underneath that was a list of banks. I Googled it and it was all those banks that had all been robbed right around the time Daddy vanished."

"So your deductive leap was to say connect those names with the robberies. That's a big swing to make with nothing else to build on. No attorney would have walked into a court with that."

"That's why I didn't say nothing to anyone. No one except Billy."

"I bet Billy recognized one of those names since he was a Tri-Comm guard, didn't he? That gave him access to the security codes to get into homes."

Billy shrugged. "No one wants to spend their life protecting shit that ain't theirs. That's all you do, work like that, looking around seeing people living better lives than what you got."

Matt hated to think Billy might have a point. If he lived through this, Matt decided he was going to reconsider working for Rachel's brother. Some of the appeal had been lost.

Matt said, "Billy have the big idea you two should destroy

property and beat up old people and cause no end of mayhem until someone gives you money? Did the thought cross your mind there might be a better way of going about all of this? Or you might have been wrong?"

"But I wasn't wrong, was I, Sheriff?" Micki said. "I figured out what no one else figured out all those years ago. Besides, were you gonna listen to me, I walked into your office and told you all this? What you'd see is the same anyone else sees looking at me: a poor white-trash kid talking shit about people better than me."

"I'd have listened to you the same way I'd have listened to anyone, Micki," Matt said. "And I would have sat you down and heard what you had to say, because that's what adults do."

Billy said, "That's bullshit. You say the universe don't care, but we still ain't ever going to be the ones who go the way the everyone else thinks we should. Soon as the world sees you ain't going to fit into its boxes, it tries to break you down. The world didn't give us no other choice."

Matt ran his hands through his hair. "People are in the hospital because of you. They will die because of your actions. You blew up someone's place of business because you were too hotheaded to find out the person you wanted to intimidate was already dead. You act like this is you two against an unfair world, but it's really just you wanting something that doesn't belong to you." He looked at Micki. "Your father robbed those banks and stole money. He'd have been just as guilty as the rest of them are. He's not noble because he's dead; he's just dead. How do you fail to see this?"

"They murdered him, Sheriff," Micki said. "My daddy wasn't a bad person. Mom always said he used to do bad things, but that was before he found out I was coming. Then these assholes talk him into doing something he probably didn't want to do, but he did it on account of me. They thought they were getting this professional thief, but Daddy was reading old books, trying to figure out how to rob banks. And what did he get for it?

What did I get for it? Nothing. The world might not care, but I do care. I care that I've never had nothing, but this bitch"—she spat the word at Iris—"she got to live off of that money."

Iris twisted her head around to glare at Micki. "I didn't live off anything from my father. The bastard cheated on my mother. She was the only decent—" Iris screamed and sprung from the floor like an animal freed from its cage, leaping at Micki. Micki jumped back, fear and shock on her face. Billy came out of his chair and swung his gun hand through the air. He caught Iris across the face, and she screamed and fell backward, hitting the wall. She clutched at her cheek as blood ran between her fingers.

Matt moved for his gun on the table. Micki came around Billy and aimed her pistol at Matt. Matt froze, staring at the gun. The girl smiled.

"You want to test the universe, Sheriff?" she said. "Really see if it don't care, Sheriff?"

Matt pulled his hands back and lowered himself back into his chair.

The front sight on the pistol had caught Iris below her right eye and had ripped down almost to her jaw. She trembled and covered her face with her hand again.

"Your father, he didn't cheat on your mother," Matt said. "Whatever happens, you should know that."

Iris didn't move. She stayed there on the floor, hiding her face, her body trembling.

Micki raised her eyebrows. "The fuck are you talking about, Sheriff?"

Matt motioned toward Iris. "She thought for years her father cheated with your mom." He looked to Micki. She had turned her own focus to Iris. "She saw him one night, outside your old place. Must have been around the time she was pregnant with you. Iris told herself father had knocked your mom up. He was just there to talk to your dad."

Iris pulled her hands back enough to show eyes welled full of tears.

"All your old man did was rob banks," Matt said. "I'm not sure if that's better or worse or what. But it's what the facts bear out."

Iris' eyes met Micki. There was a moment, a split second, where the women seemed to share a connection to one another. They both possessed with ideas of who their fathers had been. Both had been men who made choices that led them to cross paths, caused their fates to collide. Because that was how life worked, with the random intersection of lives. Matt felt the decades dividing these two women, the life experiences, the expectations that drove them at different points, those things passed through and in this second, these women understood one another.

Everything existed in that moment, and just as quickly, the moment vanished.

Micki shook her head and walked away.

"Doesn't change shit," she said. "I still want my goddamn money."

Matt slumped in his seat. "You've got no cards, Micki. I don't know how else to explain this. The money doesn't exist, and even if it did, there's no way for you to get it. Let me and Ms. Warner go. Let me take you and Billy in and we end this with no one else hurt."

"No," Micki said. "I want what's mine. That money, we'll get Billy somewhere he can record demos. Get himself a record deal." She smiled again, looking at Billy with the emotion you only get when the world hasn't worn away the pieces of you that allow that feeling to begin with.

Billy, though, he stayed dead-eyed and emotionless. Gun in hand, focused on Matt. Matt knew Billy would kill him. He hadn't missed a beat taking a swing at Iris, and she was fortunate it hadn't blinded her.

Matt took deep breaths.

"All right," he said. "What do you want to do, Micki?"

"Are you fucking dense, Sheriff?" she said. "Money. I want paid what was owed to my daddy."

"By Campbell."

"By all those fuckers. They all owe me for putting me in the shit-storm of my life. They can all fucking die and rot, but I'll get what they owe me."

"Then we'll start with Campbell. He's at the regional jail. We'll talk to him and get account numbers from him. Find out what banks he's got money in, and we'll get it out in the morning."

"You serious, Sheriff?" Micki said. Her tone vacillated between glee and suspicion. "You'll do that?"

"Yeah, I'll do that. I've got no particular inclination toward letting you two rubes kill me or Ms. Warner, and these guys are bastards anyway, so fuck it. Why not?"

Micki squealed a little with delight, jumping up and down. "Fuck yeah!" She threw her arms around Billy's neck and kissed him on the cheek. Billy betrayed no emotion. "This is it, honey. I told you we could do it."

"Yeah, you did."

Matt stood up. "Let's go."

Billy rose from his chair. "If it's all the same to you, Sheriff, I think it'll just be you and me. Micki can stay here with what's her face—"

Iris glared at him. "I've got a name, you fucking hillbilly."

Micki moved toward Iris, raising her pistol to bring it down onto the other woman. Iris saw the movement and cowered.

Billy said, "Stop."

Micki froze where she was. "She can't talk like that."

"Bitch can talk however she wants; ain't gonna matter soon, anyway. She says anything while we're gone, shoot her in the stomach. Takes a long time to die that way. You suffer like you wouldn't believe. Saw it in *Reservoir Dogs*. You bleed for a long time, and you wish to fuck you'd just die." He walked over to the bed and grabbed a pillow and threw it to Micki. "Muffle the shot with that."

Matt heard Iris swallow hard. Micki looked at the pillow, then at Billy. She nodded without an expression on her face.

Billy pointed the pistol back at Matt. "Let's do this." He grabbed Matt by the shirt collar, jerking him out of the chair, and dug the gun into the small of his back.

They walked to the door, cold beads of sweat trickling down Matt's neck, Billy pushing the gun further into Matt's back.

Billy spit out a little laugh. "You skinny as fuck, Sheriff."

"Cancer'll do that to you."

"Yeah, I've had family with it. They looked like shit right there before the end. Kinda like how you look."

At the door, Matt paused. It caught Billy off guard and he stumbled but caught himself. He pushed at Matt.

"What the fuck you waiting for?" Billy said.

"I need to know something."

"Okay."

Matt gave his head a quarter-turn. "You and Micki. That thing for real?"

Billy cocked his lips into a half smile. "It's something to do."

"You got a plan, then? What happens after all this?"

Billy shrugged. "Ain't thought that far ahead. She's a kid, and she's fun, but this is real money we're talking here. You can do a lot with real money."

"Yeah, I suppose you can."

Matt opened the hotel room door and stepped out into the hallway, Billy right behind him. They were barely past the door when Crash shot Billy with the Taser.

Chapter 35

Crash sat in the room next door, ear against the wall. Old hotel, thin walls, she made out enough to develop context and understand what they were saying. She heard the brief struggle, debated busting her way in and using surprise to her advantage, but as quickly as everything stirred to life, it settled and Crash instead took a deep breath and waited.

Patience wasn't in Crash's nature. Matt had told her this more than once, and more so now since she became chief deputy. He said patience was the greatest virtue that a cop possessed.

There was nothing even in the neighborhood of a plan before Matt knocked on the hotel door. He only told her to go into the adjoining room, listen close, play it by ear. Which was a terrible idea, Crash thought, but they also didn't have much else to work with. Next to patience, Matt said, adaptability was a cop's next best virtue.

When she heard them getting ready to leave the room, Crash crept out of her own room as silently as possible—a gift developed through years of sneaking out of her parents' house to find her way into mischief—and got herself into position.

She crouched on her belly as the door opened and the men came out. Matt exited first, followed by Billy. She was about three feet away from the door, and she hoped Billy wouldn't be looking for a tiny woman on the ground.

He wasn't.

The coiled wires sprung free from the Taser as Crash pulled the trigger, and the barbs hit Billy somewhere mid-thigh, piercing his jeans, burying into his legs.

Then the juice hit. Billy vibrated like a man possessed by the Holy Ghost, when what he was really possessed by was fifty thousand volts of electrical charge racking through his body. His teeth chattered, his eyes rolled to the back of his skull, and he dropped forward.

The dead weight caught Matt off guard, and he spun around and grabbed Billy and pivoted him toward the floor. Matt reached for Billy's gun. Billy's muscles cinched to create a vise grip on the weapon. Matt grabbed Billy's arm and slammed the man's hand against the hallway wall. Billy couldn't make a noise. Foam rolled out of his mouth. Matt pounded his hand over and over, watching the fingers loosen with each successive blow, until Billy's hand opened and the gun dropped to the floor. Matt swept it up and brought himself around and aimed for the door.

Micki stood in the hotel doorway, tears in her eyes, her own gun trembling in both hands. She made an anguished cry, a suffering wail that filled Matt's ears.

There was the gunshot, and a burning sensation erupted in the center of Matt's chest. Pure instinct, and he grabbed for it, grabbed for the source of the pain, but there was nothing to embrace. He pulled back his hand, and all he saw was the blood.

Another gunshot, and the fire inside Matt raged deeper as his feet gave out underneath him, and he slow-motion tumbled backward, stopping only when the wall met him. His vision blurred. Yet another roar of thunder, and this time he heard Micki scream.

The outline of Crash filled his line of sight. Her voice called out to him from a hundred miles away, repeating his name, then yelling something about an ambulance. His name again.

The world around him grew dark, and the sounds fuzzed

out, like lost signals from distant radio stations.
Crash said his name again.
Matt.
Matt.
Matt.

Chapter 36

When Crash had been young—not that many years ago, she supposed—and dreamed of being sheriff, this wasn't how Crash imagined it happening. That had always been the goal: to be sheriff of Parker County. Not the most glamorous of dreams, but no one ever said Charlotte Abigail Landing was the most normal or glamorous of women, and she was good with that.

The entire first week on the job, she kept going to what had been her old office, rather than the sheriff's office. To her, it was still Matt's office. Didn't matter they had already put up a new nameplate on the door. "Charlotte Landing, Acting Sheriff, Parker County."

She boxed up the few things Matt kept there and took them over to Rachel. Rachel accepted them and said thank you and politely closed the door. Crash knew Rachel's plate would be full for a while.

The county commission chewed Crash out for not following departmental protocol and not bringing backup to a hostage situation. She told them she had been going on the sheriff's orders, and if they wanted to argue about everything, to take it up with him. That shut them up quickly, and the next order of business had been to name her acting sheriff, a title she would hold on to until the election in November.

She wasn't sure what pissed everyone off so much anyway: both Billy and Micki had survived for the county attorney to file a litany of charges against both, up to and including first-degree murder following the death of Wilma Campbell. The little psychos were going to prison for a long fucking time.

The other deputies adapted quickly to her being in charge. She expected to catch more shit than she did, but they kept it all to good-natured ribbing and the occasional joke about her age. If none of them had wanted to deal with being chief deputy, they sure as fuck didn't want the headaches that came with the sheriff's badge. She still got called "Crash," but when things came through the office, they deferred to her authority. Several times, she caught them calling her "Sheriff." It sounded funny coming from their mouths, and she wasn't sure when she would get used to it. Even in town, when someone said "Sheriff," she looked for Matt but didn't find him and remembered who they were talking to now.

Iris Warner wrote her a thank-you card. It came to the sheriff's department, the script so perfect and feminine. It almost embarrassed Crash for the nearly illegible scrawl she called her own handwriting.

Crash ran into Gloria Miller while grocery shopping at Walmart. She pushed her cart through the cereal aisle, wondering who decided frosted shredded wheat needed to be blueberry flavored on top of already being frosted, when she looked up and saw Gloria. Her hair was finger-combed with gray throughout now, and her eyes swollen and puffy and dark. She stood there with her cart, looking at Crash.

They stared at one another while that damn Smash Mouth song everyone sings at karaoke played through the overhead speakers. Other shoppers moved around them.

Crash glanced into Gloria's cart: bread, lunch meat, microwave meals, and six-packs of beer.

Gloria brought her lips tight together and said, "How are you, Sheriff?"

Crash nodded. "I'm good. Yourself?"

"I'm here. You know how that goes."

"Yeah."

And then they let that uncomfortable silence sit between them for longer than they realized. Finally, Gloria said, "You have a good one, Sheriff."

"You too."

And they pushed their carts past one another and moved on with the rest of their night.

Crash drove the groceries over to Cassie Peters' place that night. It was a double-wide, this ancient thing older than Crash—much older than Crash, if she had to make a guess—with the aluminum siding peeling away like the skin on an orange. Lights were on inside, and Crash heard a TV playing as she pulled up into the driveway. She parked behind some Ford Escort sitting on two flats.

Cassie met her outside as Crash walked toward the door, holding the bags of groceries. Cassie smiled at the sight of Crash before her expression shifted to confusion.

"Hey there," Cassie said. "What are you doing here?"

Crash moved the bags in her arms. "I was at the store, realized I bought too much, thought maybe you might need it."

Cassie sucked in a few shortened breaths. She tugged at the hem of her Metallica T-shirt. "You don't have to—"

"Don't have to do a lot of things, but I do them anyway." Crash gestured with the bags again. "You wanna grab one of these? They've heavier than you'd think."

Cassie's face turned pink and her smile became awkward and she grabbed one of the bags. She snuck a fast glance inside, like a child looking for Christmas gifts.

Crash looked toward the trailer. "Parents home?"

Cassie rolled her eyes. "One's out saving her soul, and the other's one, I don't sure the bastard's got a soul to save."

There it was, the edge Crash remembered from the night at the hotel, from listening through thin walls and hearing Micki Miller, hearing all that anger. Micki, consumed with resentment for the world not being what she thought it should be. Crash knew what that anger had been like, and she knew how she had dealt with it: loud music, martial arts, and deciding to become a cop. She couldn't make the world right, not the entire world, but she could work on her part of the world.

"You want a job?" Crash said.

The words were sudden, and they caught Cassie off-guard. "A job?"

"We've got a mountain of old paperwork in the basement that needs scanned and input in the system. The clerks are all busy with everything else, so it's something you can come in and do for a few hours after school, and Saturdays if you feel industrious. It'll look good on your college application."

That last part pulled laughter from Cassie. "College application. Whatever."

Crash handed her the other bag of groceries. "You come by tomorrow afternoon and we'll get you set up scanning. Then let's talk about college."

The realization that Crash wasn't joking crept across Cassie's face. She nodded. "All right. I'll see you after school."

"Yes you will," Crash said as she got back into her truck and backed out of the driveway. Cassie watched her from the driveway until the truck was in the road and pulling away, then she went back inside.

About a month after that night at the hotel was when Rachel called Crash. She was sitting in her office—*her* office, she kept reminding herself—when her cell phone rang.

"Everything okay, Rachel?" Crash said.

"It's fine, Crash. Listen, you doing anything after work?"

"No plans at the present. Why?"

"Because he'd like to see you."

Chapter 37

Crash showed up at the front door holding flowers because she thought that was a thing you did in circumstances like this. Truth be told, she didn't know what circumstances like this were. Matt wasn't a man inclined toward receiving bouquets of flowers, but it felt like the polite thing to do.

Rachel hugged her before she had even got through the door. She took the flowers and wiped back tears. "Good to see you, Crash."

"Good seeing you too. How you holding up?"

"Good. Real good." She said it in that way meant to affirm herself more than anyone else.

There was a long pause before Crash said, "It okay if I come in?"

Rachel's face flushed with embarrassment. "I'm sorry. My brain's a million places these days. Come on in." Rachel closed the door behind Crash and led her into the kitchen.

"He's asleep on the couch," Rachel said. "His meds wear him out. He starts watching something on Netflix and then he falls asleep. I have to pause the movie as soon as he's asleep because otherwise he feels bad for sleeping. Sometimes, he's out so long, the sun goes down and he wakes up and it's nighttime and he's confused. I'm not sure always how much of the confusion is the meds and how much of it is just the exhaustion."

She rummaged through cabinets until she found a green vase

she filled with water and set the flowers in. Crash took a seat at the kitchen table.

From the refrigerator, Rachel produced a bottle of red wine. "Care for some?"

"Sure. Is it any good?"

Rachel opened the wine and poured Crash a glass. "No clue. The label's pretty, and sometimes that's all you need in life."

Crash sipped the wine. It was cold—she had read somewhere that was a no-no for reds but she didn't care—and it was sweet with a twinge of bite underneath it. She took another sip. "It's not bad."

"I guess that's all you can ask from cheap wine," Rachel said as she poured herself a glass of iced tea and sat down across from Crash. She held her glass out across the table. Crash touched the rim of her own against Rachel's.

"To drinking wine that might be shit, but not caring anyway," Crash said.

Rachel drank some of her tea and set the glass down. "Thanks for showing up in civvies."

Crash had changed into jeans and a snap-button shirt before coming over. It had been a request from Rachel, not wearing her uniform. Crash understood Rachel's reasoning.

"Not a problem," Crash said. "I got into a roll with a dude today—wanted to give me grief because he got a speeding ticket. Came by the office pissed off at the world."

"You kick his ass?"

"I told him we take a zero-tolerance attitude toward bullshit in the sheriff's department. He was limping when all was said and done, though I guess I did most of the doing, and he didn't have much to say afterward." She smiled. "Matt would have liked it."

"I'll bet he would have."

"You still on leave from the school?"

"Yes. Insurance offered to have a nurse here during the day with him, but it seems so unnecessary. One comes in during the mornings, checks in on him, but I'd rather be here in case he needs anything."

"What about you and work? You can't stay here forever."

She drank more tea. "He's scheduled for surgery in two days. Gets himself a brand new liver. Which I suppose is like a new used car; it's new to him. It'll be better than the one he's got."

"He ready for that?"

"Doesn't matter if he's ready; he's on a schedule now. They're saying if it's not now, it's too late. Might be too late anyway."

"How's he feeling about it?"

"Fine. As fine as you can, I guess. Part of me worries he doesn't care. Everything happened so fast. I don't know how many more fights he has in him."

Crash finished her wine. The last sip was strong, as though all the sediment had found its way to the bottom. Which it likely had. That was how sediment worked.

"Does he know?" she said.

Rachel lifted an eyebrow. "About what?"

"We're both smart people here, Rachel, so let's keep acting like we are."

Rachel laughed. "I haven't told him. Not yet."

"Gonna tell him?"

"When the time's right."

"Who'll decide that time?"

She shook her head. "I suppose I will. Not sure what to say to him. Not a thing I practiced or prepared for."

"He'll take it the way he takes everything."

"So goddamn stoically it makes you want to puke."

"Basically."

From the living room, a voice said, "Crash finally get her ass here?"

The women smiled at one another.

Crash called back, "No!"

There was laughter, and Matt said back, "Jesus but don't make me try to get in there. You're young and fit, and not dying, to boot. So if you please..."

Rachel shook slightly at the words. Crash stretched her arm across the table and rubbed Rachel's shoulder. Rachel's face bunched up, straining out a smile through a pained expression, working to hold back tears.

"You go deal with the asshole," Rachel said. "I've got dinner to finish."

The last time Crash had seen Matt had been at the hospital, after the shooting, and he had been unconscious. The doctors kept him sedated, unsure of how he would be when he woke up, and needing him to remain as quiet and still as possible. When he did wake up, he told Rachel he wanted no visitors. Crash had debated on showing up to the hospital unannounced, then thought the better of it, knowing Matt, even in a bed, might raise enough ruckus to make a person regret an effort toward kindness. Matt was that kind of guy.

Crash checked in with Rachel a few times a week to see how he was doing, to see how she was holding up. He was home a week before he agreed to let Crash come by. She hadn't been sure what to expect.

It might have been worse than she feared. He was propped up on the couch, sitting up but using one arm to hold himself upright. Dressed in sweatpants and a black T-shirt, and ready to be swallowed up by the clothing. His cheeks sunk deep into his face, and his eyes seemed ready to bulge free from their sockets. There was more white than dark in his hair now, longer than she had ever seen it, growing out awkwardly with points poking out everywhere. He had let a scraggly excuse for a beard grow; it was almost a checkerboard of colors. The beard might have been a saving grace since it hid the yellow in his complexion.

Matt caught her looking, not saying anything, standing in the living room entrance as if she were a child about to be admonished by a parent. He smiled and motioned to a chair. "Sit your ass down and stop staring at how bad I look."

Crash couldn't help but laugh and do as she was told. Matt snatched the remote control from the back of the couch and muted the TV. The basketball game went silent.

"Who's playing?" Crash said.

"No goddamn clue. When I fell asleep, guys were shooting each other. I wake up, it's this. How's life behind the big desk?"

"Just keeping it warm until you get back."

"I would not hold my breath on that occurring anytime soon."

"Whatever. Give you a little more time to heal up, you'll be back."

"That's real sweet of you to say, Crash, but you have no poker face whatsoever, and I saw you when you came through that door. I'm well aware I look like poorly warmed—over death. The sad thing is from how high of a peak I fell."

"It is a tragedy."

"Truly. I was so goddamn good-looking. Lucky for me, Rachel's vision isn't getting any better, so there might still be hope. You holding it all together?"

"We haven't collapsed into chaos or anarchy yet, if that's what you're asking. I've kept Parker County society from falling apart somehow."

"Good job. Guys treating you okay?"

"They're treating me like their boss, which was all I wanted. Everyone's still a smartass. You talked to Carl?"

"He's come by a few times. He wheels himself in here and gives me grief about lying around on the couch when he's out there in the world, doing things, asking when we're going fishing again—shit like that. I'm confident that Amy's glad to get him out of the house."

"No doubt. You mind I ask you a question?"

"Why'd I let him come over before you?"

"Yes."

"Because he and I have a lot of years chalked up together. Seen a fair amount together. Plus, after he got shot, I worked to be there for him. Now, he gets to be here for me. It had a lot more to do with him needing something than with you needing something. You've got plenty to juggle right now. Carl needs a thing, whatever it is. Besides, he wanted to know why it was, he got shot, he got a wheelchair and a catheter, and I got shot, now I'm getting a new liver. He doesn't think it's fair."

"Rachel told me they found a donor."

"They did. Once I got healed up enough they surmised I'll survive the surgery, they decided it might be the right time to pull this parlor trick. It seems like I'm not going to hang around much longer otherwise."

"You'll be around forever, Matt. You'll throw dirt on the graves of your enemies."

"How many people you think I've pissed off, Crash?"

"Over a lifetime, I can't say, but I imagine today alone, almost anyone you've come in contact with."

"Just as well I don't go anywhere."

A smile crossed Crash's face. "I brought you flowers. Rachel put 'em in a vase."

"Much appreciated. Everyone brought me flowers and houseplants for a while. We managed to kill most of 'em off, so we'll see how these do." Matt stretched his legs out and brought his feet out onto the coffee table. He wore house slippers. "They gonna do a special election, fill the office?"

"Doesn't seem like it. Sounds like the plan is to wait until next November. County doesn't want to deal with the expense, and I can't say I blame 'em."

"You gonna run?"

Crash shrugged a shoulder. Wanted to come off half-hearted and disinterested. "Maybe. I like the office. The space, if not the title. The view's nice."

"The view's terrible. All you can see is Serenity."

"If you didn't know what you were talking about, that would sound great. But yeah, I'll run. I hear there are a few folks talking about throwing hats in there. There're pocketbooks opening up, offering to help out. I'm not sure everyone enjoys having a female sheriff barely old enough to drink."

"Especially one who looks like she's missing a sophomore English class. Regardless of how badass she is with a stun gun." Matt reached to an end table for a glass and drank some water. "Anyone from within the department talking about running?"

"No one wants the headache."

"It is a fucking headache, ain't it?"

"I got people showing up all hours of the day to bitch and complain about every little goddamn thing you can imagine. I fantasize on a daily basis about how satisfying it'd be just to punch 'em in the mouth. Line 'em up one by one and hit 'em, and then let 'em get on with whatever they want done."

"But first, a punch."

"Definitely."

"But it's still a great job, isn't it?"

"Completely. Which is why I'll be stupid and try to fight for it."

"What if you don't?"

"I might find out about annoying 'em over at the state police. I'm sure me and Jackie Hall would get along great."

"You likely would. Though he may not be the level one jack hole I've always made him out to be."

"I didn't figure he was. You, on the other hand—"

"Total level one jack hole. All day, every day."

Crash didn't stay long. She said something about having somewhere she needed to be, but Crash knew she couldn't lie for shit, and Matt smiled as she said it. He was tired anyway. Rachel walked her to the door. By the time Rachel came back, Matt was asleep.

Rachel poured herself more tea and went out onto the back deck. The air was getting cool. Seasons would change soon.

She wanted a cigarette but shook the feeling off. She had gotten rid of the pack she kept hidden near the bushes two weeks ago. Kept telling herself it was a bad habit anyway.

She considered calling the school tomorrow, asking when she could start back. She needed to be there for Matt, but Crash was right that she needed to be there for herself also. She realized sometimes she was a woman who'd built her identity on the backs of the men she attracted. It was a nasty trait, something a lot of women did, she thought. She remembered her mother having gone through a series of husbands—her father was the third of five—before finally ending up by herself, dying alone, angry and bitter because none of those marriages had brought her the happiness she thought she had deserved, that she believed was her right.

Rachel had been in the hospital while her mother's heart gave out and she died. Rachel had fancied the concept that her mother had died of a broken heart, but that gave her mother too much credit. That implied a love and compassion the old woman hadn't always been capable of, and that had somehow both attracted and driven away five husbands and countless other men who had been lucky enough to escape.

She didn't hear the door slide open, so lost in her thoughts, and it startled her when Matt slipped into the lounge chair beside her. The temperature was mild, but he had put on a heavy sweatshirt. She moved to get up.

"What are you doing out here?" she said. "You'll freeze yourself to death."

Matt took her hand and said, "Sit back down. I'm fine. Let's be here for a moment."

Rachel considered this, then lowered herself back into the chair. Matt didn't let go of her hand, and their fingers intertwined with one another.

Matt said, "What are you out here thinking about?"

"Not much. That we should get some new bushes in the yard."

"We could do that."

"But if we move to Charleston, how much money do we want to sink into this place? We'll never get all of that back in the selling price."

"No, but sometimes it's nice just to have pretty things to look at." He gave Rachel's hand a small squeeze. "With that in mind, we could put up a big privacy fence and you could sunbathe naked."

"Pervert."

"Guilty as charged. Though I bet we could get a privacy fence in Charleston too."

"Are you giving it some thought now?"

"Some. Your brother keeping the offer open?"

"Always. He'd love to have us closer anyway. It'd be more money than you make now, and regular hours. You'd be home at five every night. You wouldn't be out at all hours dealing with criminals and whatnot."

"It's still working for a security company. I'd be catching criminals in the act."

"You wouldn't be like a security guard or anything. You'd be in the office. You could wear a tie every day."

"You are not doing a grandiose job of selling me on this."

"I don't suppose I am."

There was a pause.

Matt said, "Once the surgery's over and we figure out whether I'm going to live or not, let's talk to him. See what the doctors say, and then we can see about heading down that way."

"Good. Thank you."

Another squeeze. "Anytime, honey."

Another pause. Rachel said, "Matt?"

"Yes, honey?" His voice sounded thick and sleepy. His head had drifted back, his eyes closed, facing toward the purpling nighttime sky.

Rachel squeezed his hand. "I'm pregnant."

JAMES D.F. HANNAH is the Shamus Award-winning author of the Henry Malone novels, as well as the novel *The Righteous Path*. A native of eastern Kentucky and southern West Virginia, Hannah was an award-winning former journalist and columnist before moving into governmental public relations. He lives with entirely too many cats in Louisville, Kentucky.

On the following pages are a few
more great titles from the
Down & Out Books publishing family.

For a complete list of books and to
sign up for our newsletter,
go to DownAndOutBooks.com.

Roughhouse
Jeffery Hess

Down & Out Books
May 2021
978-1-64396-132-3

If Scotland Ross doesn't get $100,000 fast, his wife will die.

A quick heist of a Tampa casino may save her life, while dooming him to life in prison if caught. Scotland never expected his trusted accomplice to go rogue and turn against him.

Betrayal, smoking guns, and a future strangled in revenge's cold grip make it a rough trip home. And the next day, things get worse.

Brand New Dark
A Bishop Rider Book
Beau Johnson

Down & Out Books
July 2021
978-1-64396-221-4

Bishop Rider Lives! And for a dead man, he's been busy. His story and the parts of it yet to be told being what populates *Brand New Dark*. Unseen moments pulled from between the pages of *A Better Kind of Hate*, *The Big Machine Eats*, and *All of Them to Burn*. Twenty-five new tales that bridge what came before and expand upon what can only come after.

Come, see what happened in-between.

Come, see how he made them burn.

To Bring My Shadow
Matt Phillips

All Due Respect, an imprint of
Down & Out Books
July 2021
978-1-64396-222-1

A haunting, hardboiled tale that follows detective Frank "Slim Fat" Pinson and his partner as they try to unravel the vexing mystery surrounding a who-done-it drug murder in San Diego, *To Bring My Shadow* is the first detective novel from acclaimed pulp writer Matt Phillips.

Meet a fascinating detective of indefensible fault, immense morality, and incalculable demise.

S-10 to Valhalla
Ken Teutsch

Shotgun Honey, an imprint of
Down & Out Books
July 2021
978-1-64396-113-2

It's Saturday, and Nashville lowlife Jake Croom needs money for the beer joints. But his seemingly straightforward plan to steal some sends him ricocheting through the lives of everyone from bat-wielding grandmothers to down-and-out typesetters to inadvertent Robert E. Lee impersonators, violently knocking them all into various unexpected pockets in life's pool table.

Meanwhile Jake, fortified by tequila, unidentified pharmaceuticals and a thirty-five-dollar pistol, caroms toward his own final collision with a counterfeit Valkyrie and a bona fide hail of bullets.

Lightning Source UK Ltd.
Milton Keynes UK
UKHW011408241121
394516UK00001B/219